I0762649

ATLAS *of Prehistoric* ANIMALS

Albatros

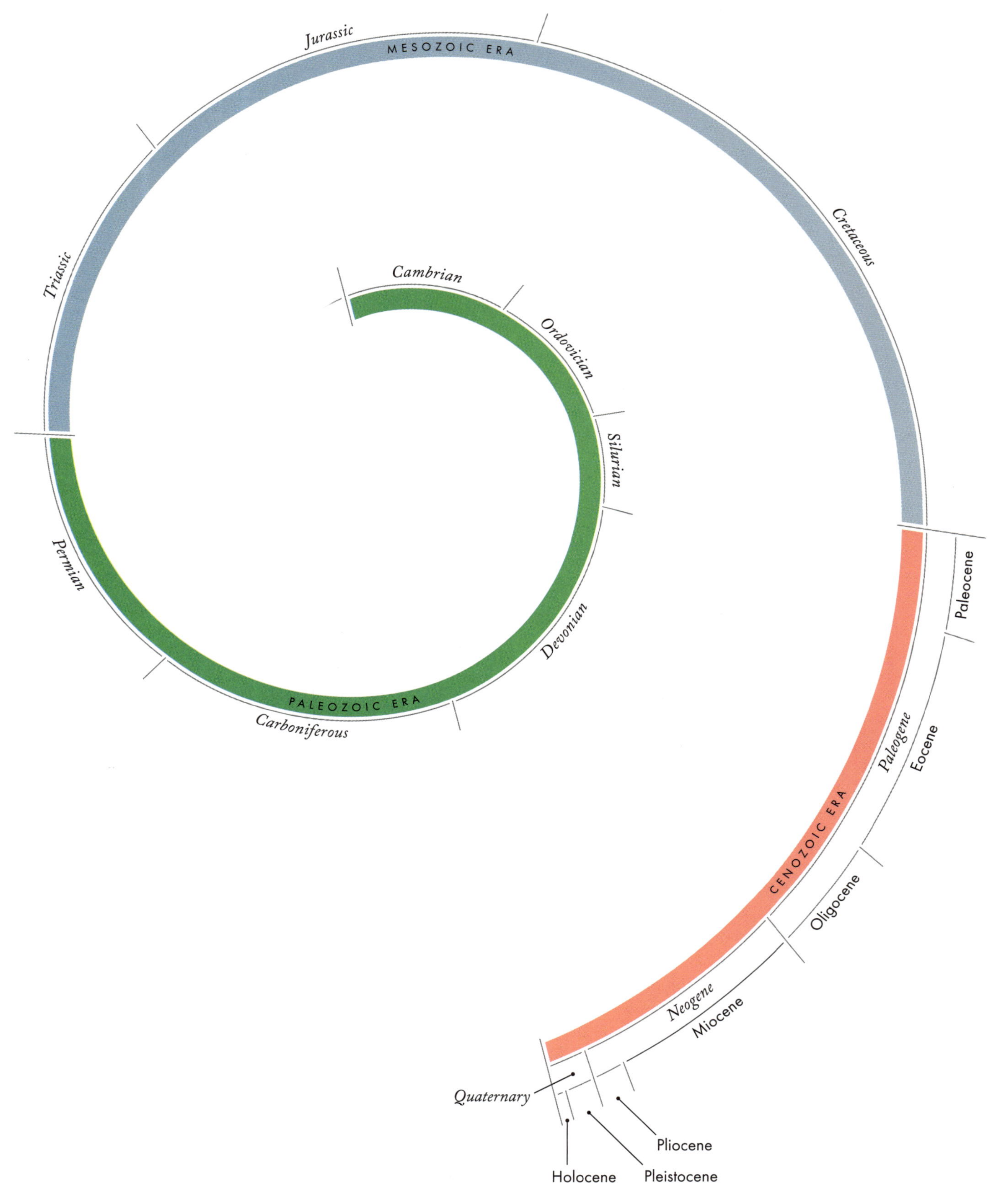

PALEOZOIC ERA						MESOZOIC ERA			CENOZOIC ERA						
Cambrian	*Ordovician*	*Silurian*	*Devonian*	*Carboniferous*	*Permian*	*Triassic*	*Jurassic*	*Cretaceous*	*Paleogene*			*Neogene*		*Quaternary*	
									Paleocene	Eocene	Oligocene	Miocene	Pliocene	Pleistocene	Holocene
538–485 MYA	485–443 MYA	443–419 MYA	419–358 MYA	358–298 MYA	298–251 MYA	251–201 MYA	201–145 MYA	145–66 MYA	66–56 MYA	56–33.9 MYA	33.9–23 MYA	23–5.3 MYA	5.3–2.5 MYA	2.58–0.01 MYA	0.01–0 MYA

Contents

Uintatherium anceps
(Eocene)

Our fascination with prehistoric times and how life has evolved on Earth reflects our desire to find our roots – to understand where we come from and where we're headed. For almost two centuries, people have been researching and sharing the results of paleontology: the branch of science concerned with the fossils of animals and plants. This book offers an exciting selection of extinct animals, dating back to when life first evolved on our planet.

Earth began forming about 4,600 **m**illion **y**ears **a**go (MYA), giving us a vast history to explore. Regardless of how life began, fossil finds have confirmed that there was life on Earth starting around 3,900 MYA. Organisms visible to the naked eye (called *macroscopic* organisms) appeared around 600 MYA. We know little about these organisms (called Ediacaran fauna), due to preservation problems. Everything changed around 540 MYA, with the start of the Cambrian Period, when many different organisms began forming hard structures like shells and skeletons that could be fossilized. We have records of almost all known biological strains from this time, although it represents only a fraction of what has been fossilized.

There are tens of millions of different species of organisms today. This is just an estimate because there are so many different types of organisms, such as insects, bacteria, and protists (a type of tiny living thing, or *microorganism*) that it's impossible to count them all! Despite this, it is estimated that about 0.5 percent of the species that existed during the Cambrian Period still exist today, suggesting that the average lifespan of a species is 2.5 million years and that there are currently around 10 million species. We humans (*homo sapiens*) have been around for around 400,000 years.

Preservation of the remains of prehistoric life is difficult. What we have evidence of now – by way of fossils, for example – is only a small fraction of what used to exist. As we examine the first million or so preserved species on Earth, we should remember that some lifeforms cannot be preserved in any way, shape, or form.

Paleontologists are scientists who study animal fossils. Using only a small fraction of what used to exist in past ecosystems, they can reconstruct what animals from the deep past looked like. Many of the successful reconstructions of animals you will see in this publication are based on only certain body parts that have been preserved.

This book contains a variety of information about vertebrates whose skeletons don't last long after death. As a result, most of what we find are just bones or pieces of bones. For example, shark teeth are often the only part of the shark that is preserved. It's rare for the entire skeleton of a cartilaginous fish (e.g., sharks and rays) to be preserved, but it does happen. Preservation also has time limitations. The further back in time we go, the less original information we have about fossils, and the fewer fossils there are. Even with these limitations, though, there are still way more fossilized species and individual animals than can be covered in one book. Scientists are constantly discovering new information about extinct organisms, and sometimes this changes their view of them. This book describes many animals you probably already know about from other books or media. Readers hoping to read about widely known (and often misrepresented) extinct fauna – such as *Tyrannosaurus*, *Megalodon*, and *Smilodon* – will not be disappointed.

As the old saying goes, "Blood is thicker than water," meaning that the strongest ties are those among families. This is reflected in this book's focus on past vertebrates – the large group of animals with spines in their backs, including mammals, birds, reptiles, amphibians, and fish. We focus on animals that are the ancestors of today's vertebrates, as well as interesting invertebrates (animals without spines). For example, trilobites have been studied by scientists for centuries, and they've become a symbol of the Paleozoic Era.

This book will introduce you to a range of invertebrates and vertebrates that lived from the early Paleozoic Era to the last Ice Age, about 125,000 years ago. We'll look at aquatic arthropods (invertebrate animals) like Eurypterids and Radiodonts, plus the mysterious – and rarely mentioned – *Hallucigenia* from the Cambrian Period. You'll learn about well-known dinosaurs, their modern-day descendants (birds), and a variety of reptiles. We'll also explore a wide range of mammals, from the last mass extinction to the present day – which includes us!

Many discoveries of ancient creatures are in pieces or fragments. So, to give the public a better understanding of what prehistoric creatures looked like, scientists create visualizations. They use schematic drawings similar to construction blueprints. Scientists have knowledge of the environment, soft tissue, and even behavior of the creature, which they share with an artist to create an impression of a long-gone world. While the artist must have artistic talent and a vivid imagination, they also need an understanding of anatomy, various environments, and animal behavior. The scientist's job, then, is to make sure the artwork is true to life, to the best of their understanding.

The illustrator of this book, Petr Modlitba, has created stunning recreations of fossilized creatures, both familiar and lesser-known. His illustrations transport us back to prehistoric times. And for Czech and Slovak readers who grew up admiring famous Czech painter Zdeněk Burian's depictions of the prehistoric world, these illustrations also bring back fond memories. Our artist humbly acknowledges Burian's influence on his work, and is proud to present it as a tribute to the master.

In closing, I'd like to clarify the difference between an archeologist and a paleontologist. Both of us dig in the ground in search of old things, but while an archeologist only studies human history dating back tens of thousands of years, a paleontologist studies everything else, dating back to the dawn of our planet. So if you're out and about and you find a fossil, let us paleontologists know about it instead of the archeologists. That way, they won't have to pass the tip along to us.

Martin Mazuch
Institute of Geology and Palaeontology, Faculty of Science, Charles University, Prague

HALLUCIGENIA SPARSA

Paleozoic Era · Cambrian

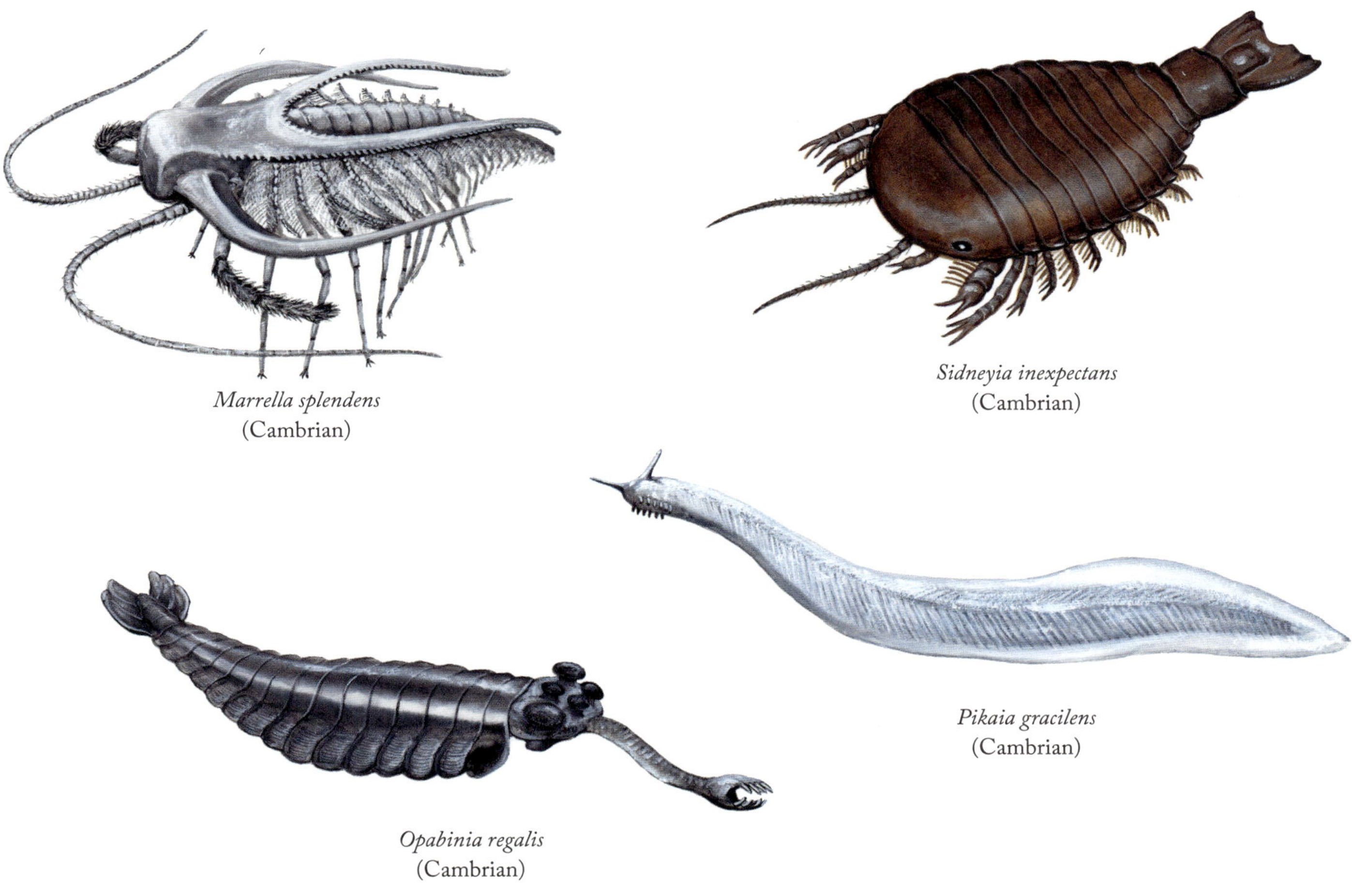

Marrella splendens
(Cambrian)

Sidneyia inexpectans
(Cambrian)

Pikaia gracilens
(Cambrian)

Opabinia regalis
(Cambrian)

LENGTH: *0.1–1.3 inches*

The origins of life on Earth are shrouded in mystery. Scientists still debate what sparked the first cell and why cells grouped together, leading to multicellular organisms – living things made of many cells working together. These organisms evolved over time and gave rise to all the fascinating creatures from prehistory up to the present day. One remarkable prehistoric creature was a very strange animal called *Hallucigenia*.

In Latin, *Hallucigenia* means "caused by hallucinations" – a fitting name for this strange extinct creature discovered by English paleontologist Simon Conway Morris in 1977. Its odd appearance, resembling a walking hairbrush, made it immediately stand out. Today, three species of this genus have been found in British Columbia in Canada, China, and various other places around the prehistoric oceans of the world – wherever conditions were ideal for fossil formation.

Hallucigenia lived during the Cambrian Period of the Paleozoic Era, about 510–520 million years ago. It was a small creature, measuring between 0.2 and two inches in length. For a long time, scientists had difficulty understanding the creature, as they couldn't tell which direction it moved or where its head even was.

And there were many other questions about *Hallucigenia*. For instance, was it related to an animal group called Onychophora? Or was it a distant ancestor of modern arthropods? Today, it belongs to its own group, called Panarthropoda. Scientists now believe that *Hallucigenia* had eight pairs of thin legs and seven pairs of spines on its back. It likely moved around on the ocean floor.

In 2015, Martin Smith from the University of Cambridge and Jean-Bernard Caron from the University of Toronto and the Royal Ontario Museum solved the greatest mystery surrounding *Hallucigenia* when they at last succeeded in locating the site of its head. Using an electron microscope, they discovered its eyes and its mouth, which was lined with teeth. They figured out that the end of the body previously thought to be its head was not part of the body at all but was actually part of something that happened after its death. Even with all the discoveries we've made, there's still so much to learn about the beginnings of life on Earth.

AEGIROCASSIS BENMOULAI

Paleozoic Era · Ordovician

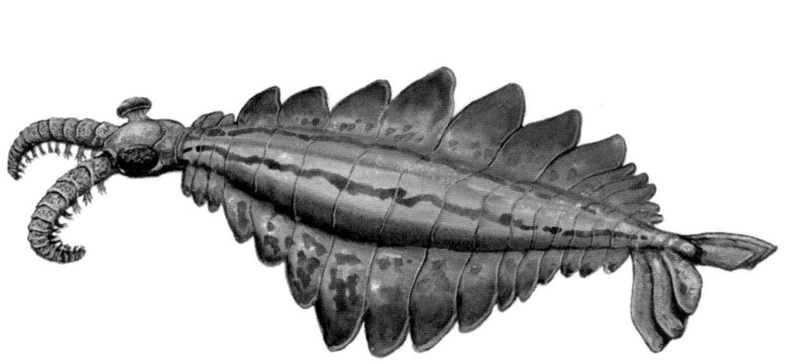

Anomalocaris canadensis
(Cambrian)

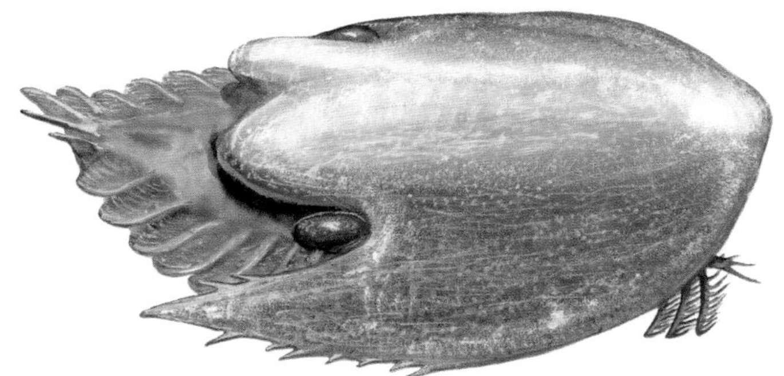

Cambroraster falcatus
(Cambrian)

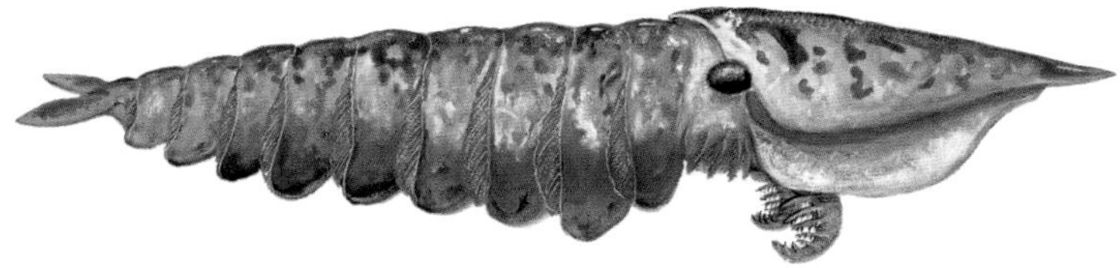

Hurdia victoria
(Cambrian)

LENGTH: *Over 6 feet*
WEIGHT: *90–440 pounds*

Most giant aquatic vertebrates feed by filtering the water around them. This includes sharks, other fish, and mammals. Invertebrates, though, first developed this way of feeding long before any of these other animals. Recently, the oldest example of this type of feeding was discovered.

Filter-feeding is a common trait in sea sponges, sea cucumbers, and jellyfish. One of the very oldest known filter-feeders is *Aegirocassis benmoulai*, a strange-looking creature that is the only known representative of its genus. It had 11 segments and its body was lined with pairs of flaps that could do many things. On the front of its trunk was a long, pointy helmet. Its eyes were not preserved in fossils, but they likely stuck out from the sides of its head. The most interesting part was its mouth and the amazing filtering device next to it. This device had seven flaps of different sizes and was covered in spines for filtering plankton.

In 2011, a fossil collector named Mohamed Ben Moula discovered a three-dimensional fossil of an arthropod in Fezouata, Morocco. To honor its finder, the species was named after him. The genus name, *Aegirocassis*, means "Aegir's Helmet" – a reference to Norse mythology, with Aegir being a supernatural personification of the sea. Seeing the importance of his find, Ben Moula contacted paleontologist Peter Van Roy. After hundreds of hours of work, Van Roy's team reconstructed the creature and provided a scientific description. At nearly 6.5 feet long, *Aegirocassis benmoulai* was one of the largest predators of its time. It was an anomalocarid, an order of mostly predators, and it was unique in its size and filter-feeding. Evolutionary pathways are fascinating to study, and this species shows that some pathways were taken by certain animals much sooner than scientists previously thought. In its time and ecosystem, *Aegirocassis benmoulai* held the role held today by large cetaceans (marine mammals such as whales, dolphins, porpoises, and narwhals).

CAMEROCERAS TRENTONENSE

Paleozoic Era · Ordovician

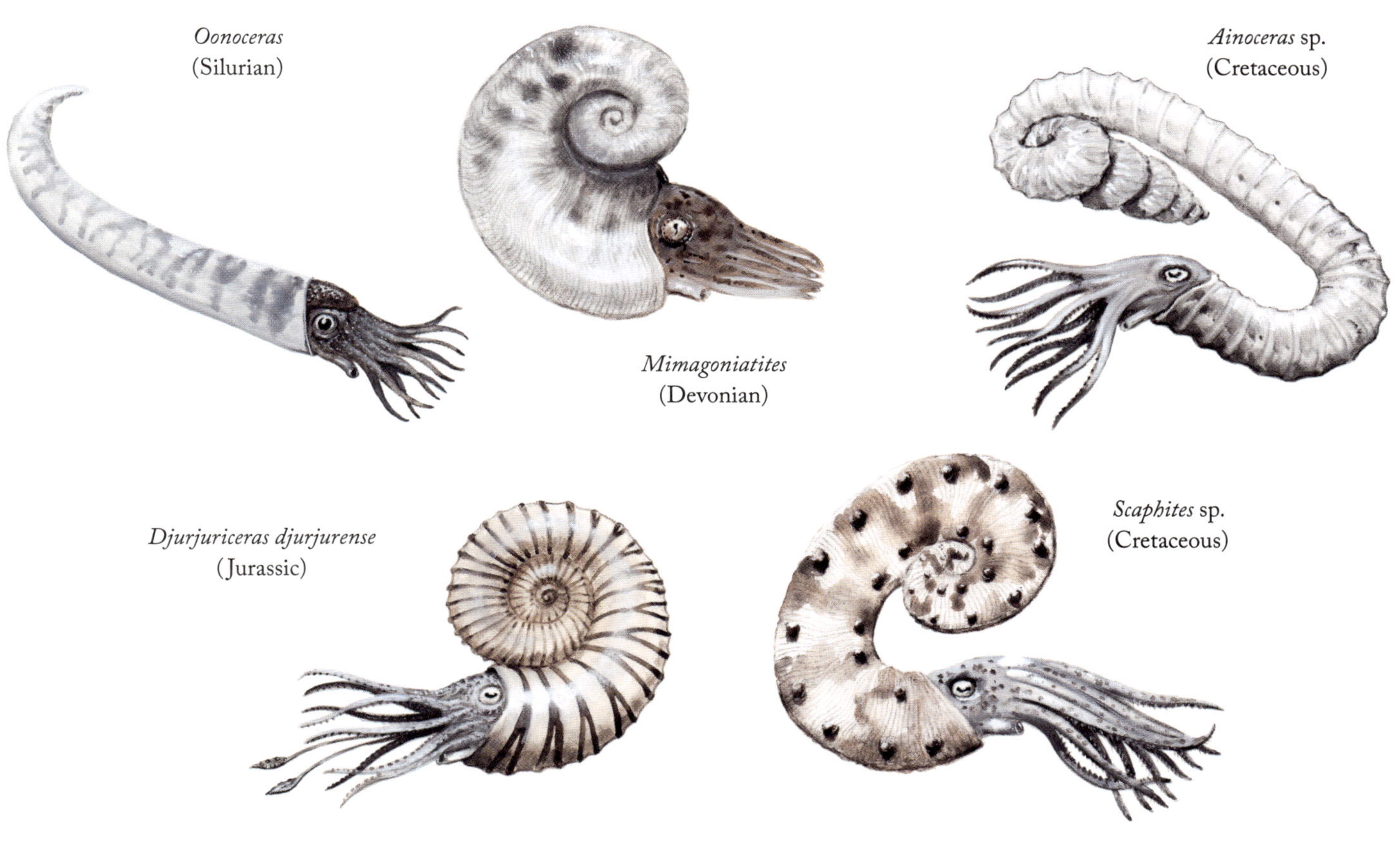

SHELL LENGTH: *Over 33 feet*
WEIGHT: *220–550 pounds*

We've all heard fantastical stories of ships being attacked by giant squids and octopuses, but there is no evidence that this kind of thing has ever happened. However, we do know that a cephalopod of the genus *Cameroceras* had a shell up to 33 feet long! Even though only fragments of the shells remain, paleontologists can tell us a lot about this creature. With its cone-shaped shell, it was a top predator in the oceans of its time. It likely ate large trilobites and eurypterids, and may have even hunted its own species. We think it had a soft body inside a hard shell, with an unknown number of tentacles (most likely ten).

Cameroceras moved up and down by using pressure in the chambers of its shell. It was even strong enough to break the tough shell of Megalograptus, a distant relative of today's arachnids (a group that includes spiders and scorpions). Megalograptus was about three feet long and its body was equipped with dangerous pincers 1.5 feet long. It may have looked like a scorpion, but it lacked a venomous spike at the end of its tail. Its claws had menacing spines, which it used to catch prey and sift through sand.

One of the most famous fossils of all time is the ammonite shell. Ammonites lived in the ocean for an incredibly long time – from 409 million years ago to 66 million years ago, shortly after the dinosaurs went extinct. Ammonites evolved quickly and were found all around the world, making them a great "index fossil" – a way to tell what period of time something else is from. The biggest ammonite shells were 6.5 feet in diameter. Even more impressive is the small one-inch shell that was found in amber that was about 1 million years old!

In ancient times, Ammonite fossils were well-known and highly regarded. During the Middle Ages, especially in Anglo-Saxon culture, they were believed to have magical powers that could protect against lightning and witchcraft. The shell of *Cameroceras* was also thought to be the horn of the mythical unicorn.

JAEKELOPTERUS RHENANIAE

Paleozoic Era · Devonian

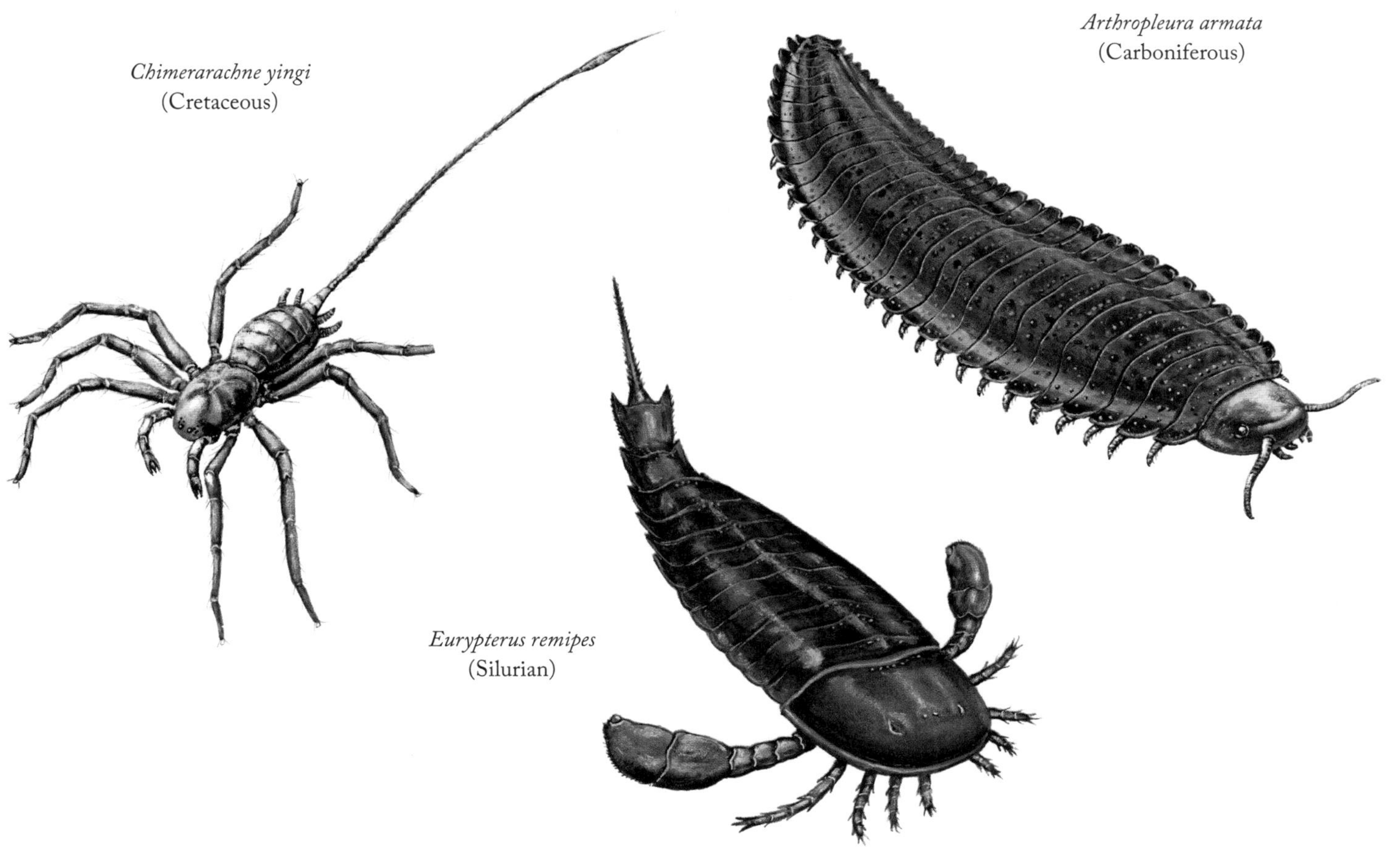

LENGTH: *Up to 8 feet*
WEIGHT: *400 pounds*

Arthropoda (arthropods), which includes the very successful and highly diverse class Insecta (insects), as well as arachnids and crustaceans, is the most diverse and numerous phylum of living organisms. Before arthropods conquered the land, they were masters of the water.

Jaekelopterus, the largest known arthropod, is a distant relative of the scorpion and is classified as a cephalopod. Its impressive claws were almost eight feet long, and its pointed tail may have been armed with a poisonous spine. Its body was protected by a carapace and it was a hunter, living on the seabed. Research published in 2020 suggests that it was able to breathe air too, allowing it to live on land as well.

Arthropods on land were no joke in terms of size. Their increased size during the Paleozoic Era can likely be attributed to the higher oxygen levels in the atmosphere then. The biggest terrestrial arthropod of all time is *Arthropleura*, which was plentiful 300 million years ago in warm marshlands. All that remains of it now, though, are pieces of its trunk joints and other fossilized remains. Even so, we can guess that it was a millipede, likely up to eight feet long, with over 30 pairs of legs, and its footprints were 1.5 feet wide. It was probably one of the first plant-eaters to inhabit the primeval rainforest. It might have been venomous and might have defended itself by raising the front of its trunk.

Spiders, which are also arthropods, can be intimidating, even though they don't grow to be giants. Scientists recently discovered a species of spider, about 100 million years old, that was preserved in amber in Myanmar. It's only 0.1 inches long, yet it looks quite scary! Its Latin name is *Chimerarachne*, which is inspired by the Chimera, a mythological creature made up of parts from different animals. This amazing find helps us understand how spiders have evolved over time. The spider's 0.2-inch tail may have been used to help it explore its environment. It's generally thought that the size of arthropods is determined by the amount of oxygen in the atmosphere. Another hypothesis suggests that Earth was rid of giant insects by insect-eating amphibians and, later, birds.

DUNKLEOSTEUS TERELLI

Paleozoic Era · Devonian

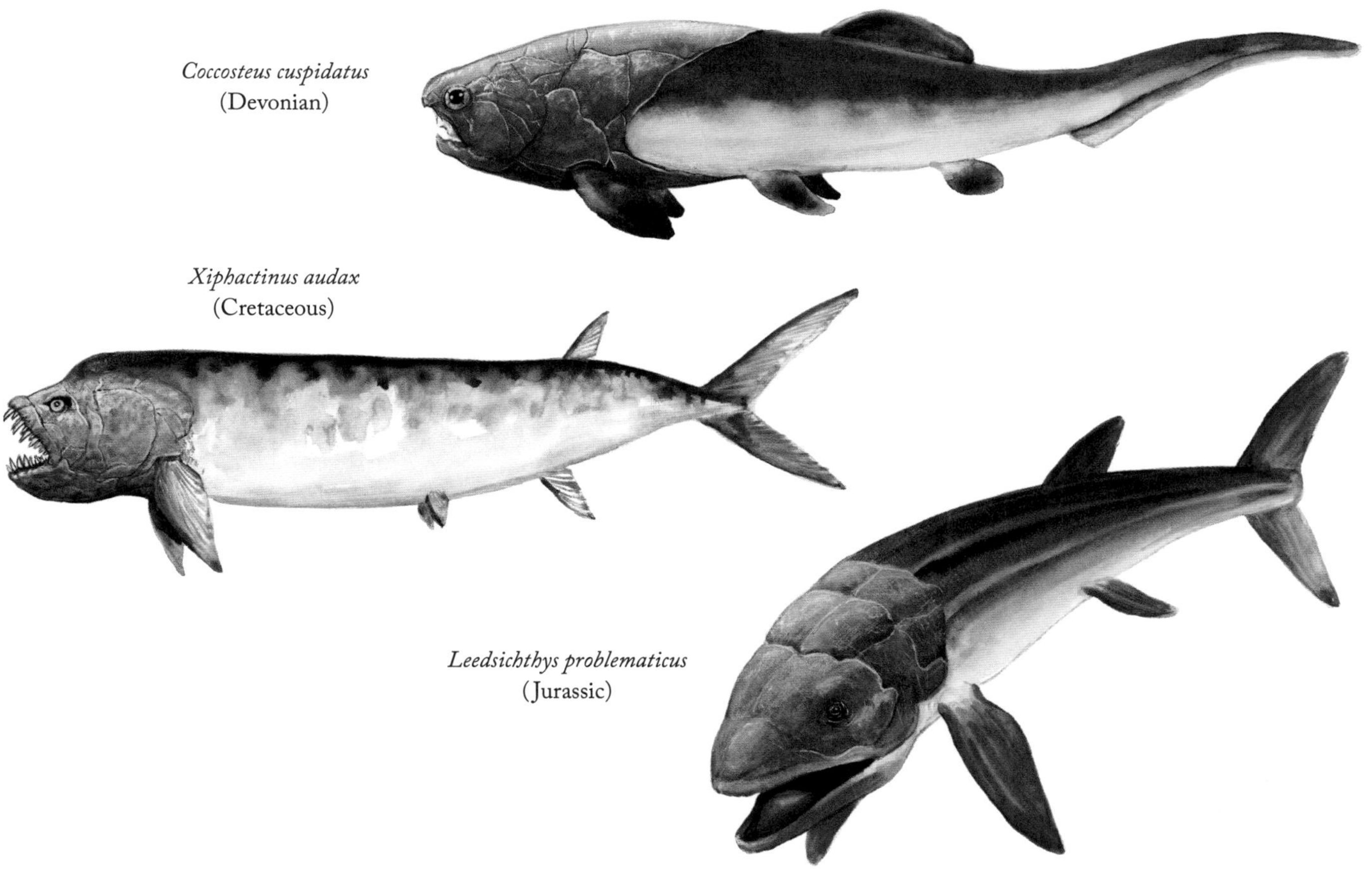

LENGTH: *13–32 feet*
WEIGHT: *1–4 tons*

Fish came to become the top predators in the ancient ocean. And at the top of the food chain was the armored *Dunkleosteus*, a prehistoric vertebrate with powerful jaws. *Dunkleosteus*, part of the placoderm class, is an ancestor of the fish we know today. Scientists have identified nine species of *Dunkleosteus*. It was named after paleontologist David Dunkle of the Cleveland Museum and means "Dunkle's bone." *Dunkleosteus* was around 33 feet long and weighed up to four tons – which is as much as a car!

On its head and feet, *Dunkleosteus* had a bony "cephalothoracic carapace" – an armor-like covering like those on turtles and crabs. Scientists are most fascinated by its mighty jaws, which had bony spikes instead of teeth. These had one of the strongest grips ever found in the animal kingdom, similar to that of a large crocodile or the famous *Tyrannosaurus*. It could open its jaws quickly, creating a suction that pulled its food into its enormous mouth. This was accompanied by a powerful and swift bite, making it practically impossible for its prey to escape. Since it only crushed its food, rather than chewing it, we can assume it gagged a lot.

It has even proven possible to identify the petrified vomit of *Dunkleosteus*. This creature likely ate anything living nearby, including cephalopods with tough shells and the early relatives of sharks. Eventually, though, the shark became the dominant predator in the environment, replacing *Dunkleosteus*.

Dunkleosteus was much smaller than *Leedsichtys problematicus*, the largest fish known from all geological periods. *Leedsichtys* was up to 52 feet long and lived in the oceans of the world during the middle Jurassic Period of the Mesozoic Era, around 170 million years ago. The name *Leedsichthys* honors Alfred N. Leeds, who discovered a fossil of this fish near Peterborough, England, in 1886. Its remains were so incomplete that it was hard to determine its shape and size. *Leedsichthys* filtered water with its big mouth and ate plankton, similar to the giant shark and, later, cetaceans. Its vastness notwithstanding, this fish became a prey, not least of Pliosaurus, a predatory marine reptile. A certain fossil found in England indicates that it was attacked but later recovered, suggesting that *Leedsichthys* may have served its predators as an ongoing food source.

MEGANEURA MONYI

Paleozoic Era · Carboniferous

Stenodictya lobata
(Carboniferous)

Meganeura monyi
(Carboniferous)

LENGTH: *2–2.3 feet*
WEIGHT: *100–150 grams*

Insects are hands down the most plentiful and diverse group of animals in the world today, with more than a million species identified so far. It's no surprise, then, that insects evolved long ago in prehistory. The most fascinating evidence of the past of insects has been found in amber, which is fossilized tree resin that has kept insects practically intact. With the help of modern technology, researchers have made some incredible findings by studying these samples.

Even so, one of the most important insect fossils – the first evidence of insect life in the Paleozoic Era – was found not in resin but in coal, in a mine in France in the 1880s. It was the fossil of a giant extinct dragonfly with an incredible wingspan of over 2.5 feet named Meganisoptera. This order included *Meganeura monyi* – the largest known flying insect of all time. Evidence from France and the United Kingdom tells us that it flew and hunted over Europe 300 million years ago. Scientists have long wondered why this insect could grow to be so big. It seems that the composition of the air in the Paleozoic Era, with up to 30 percent oxygen in the atmosphere, created a different atmospheric pressure than what we have today. In 2018, a team of French, Czech, and US scientists studied various fossils and determined that Meganeura, the ancient dragonfly, likely did not have the same impressive flying abilities as modern dragonflies. Instead, it likely flew in a straight line and stayed close to the ground to hunt.

Thanks to incredibly well-preserved fossils, scientists have been able to make surprising breakthroughs with modern methods. In 2012, they were even able to recreate the sound of an insect that lived 165 million years ago! This insect was a small orthopteran called *Archaboilus musicus*, a distant ancestor of crickets, locusts, and grasshoppers. It made a creaking noise that was likely used to attract females. This is why the researchers who discovered this noise nicknamed it the "Jurassic Love Song."

Scientists have discovered a variety of creatures from the prehistoric world trapped in amber, such as spiders, reptiles, and frogs. In Myanmar, a country in Southeast Asia, even more unique findings have been made, like ticks, centipedes, and termites. It's clear that the prehistoric insect world still has many secrets to reveal.

TRILOBITOMORPHA

Paleozoic Era · Cambrian – Permian

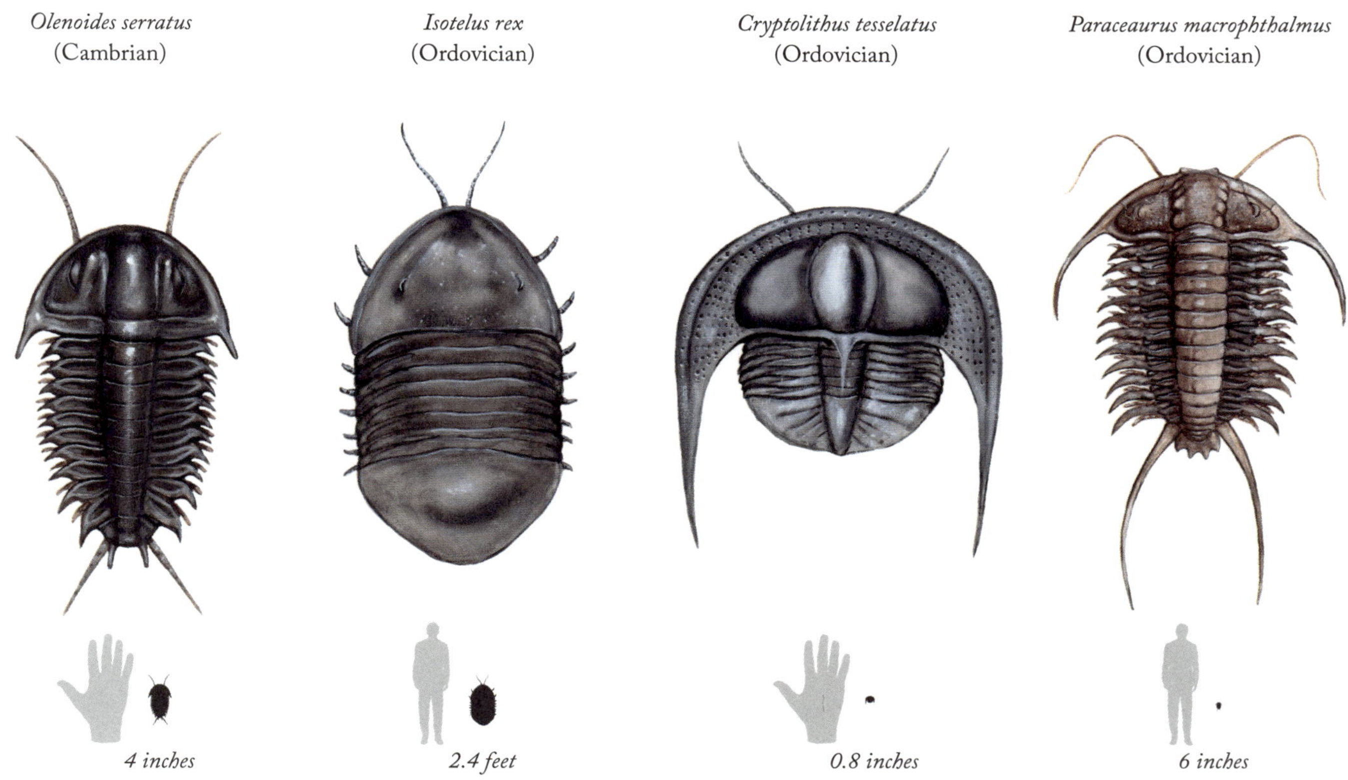

LENGTH: *0.12–18 inches*
WEIGHT: *Up to 100 pounds*

Trilobites are one of the most recognizable prehistoric creatures. They are often seen as a symbol of the Paleozoic Era, the earliest of three eras in Earth's history when life began to evolve. They lived for almost 300 million years, which is more than 30 percent longer than the time the dinosaurs were around!

Trilobites were prehistoric arthropods with three lobes – one in the middle and two on the sides – that gave them the *tri* (meaning *three*) in their name. They lived in the ocean, some at the bottom and some floating on the top. With so many fossils found, it's clear they were very abundant. To survive, they evolved into many different species – some ate plankton, some were active hunters. Scientists have already discovered over 15,000 trilobite species, and this number just keeps growing.

The variety of trilobites is evident in their size: the smallest known species were just a few inches long, while the largest, *Isotelus rex*, was over two feet long. *Redlichia rex*, which is around one foot long and found off the coast of southern Australia, is notable for its large, spiky spines, which likely protected it from predators. Trilobites were prey for cephalopods or larger arthropods of the genus *Anomalocaris*, some of the earliest large predators on Earth.

As trilobites have no living relatives, we know little about their behavior. But fossils can tell us more. Recently, Estonian scientists found a 530-million-year-old trilobite fossil with well-preserved eyes – the earliest eyes ever found in a fossil! Tiny trilobite eggs have also been discovered, and their position on the body shows us that they reproduced through external fertilization. In addition, fossils from southern Morocco provide evidence of trilobites engaging in social behavior in formations.

We've learned a lot about trilobites, but much about how they lived remains a mystery. The biggest mystery of all is why they went extinct – we still don't know why. The closest living creature to the trilobite is the horseshoe crab, an arthropod that's been around since the Paleozoic Era, making it what is called a "living fossil."

GERROTHORAX PULCHERRIMUS

Mesozoic Era · Triassic

LENGTH: *3 feet*
WEIGHT: *Unknown*

One of the largest changes to occur in the evolution of vertebrates was their transition to land and their gradual mastery of this element. The process began with lobe-finned fish, whose fins gradually changed into limbs.

Vertebrates didn't start appearing on land until around 360 million years ago. Their direct ancestor was probably a fish called *Tiktaalik*, which was found in northern Canada on Ellesmere Island in 2004 by Chicago paleontologist Neil Shubin – during his lunch break. *Tiktaalik* takes its name from a word used by the Inuit, the original people of this region, meaning "big fish." It had gills and small, primitive lungs, allowing it to move around on land. Unlike modern fish, it could turn its head, making it easier to hunt prey from below the surface of shallow pools. *Tiktaalik* was about six feet long and had a unique skeletal structure that reflected the gradual evolution of its neck and limbs.

Diplocaulus lived on Earth between 252 million and 299 million years ago. This amphibian was well known for its boomerang or arrow-shaped head. Scientists don't agree on why it had this shape. Was it to attract mates or to scare off rivals? Or was it used as a fin to defend against predators? Whatever the case, the head shape definitely made it hard for predators to swallow this creature. *Diplocaulus* was about three feet long and ate fish. Its fossils have been found in North America and, surprisingly, Morocco.

The younger amphibian *Gerrothorax pulcherrimus* was discovered in Greenland, inhabiting it around 210 million years ago. Back then, the landscape was filled with shallow pools and warm lakes. Since then, its fossils have been found all over the world. It was about three feet long, with a very flat body and eyes on top of the head. Like *Diplocaulus*, it hunted fish, but in a unique way. It could open the top half of its head to a 50-degree angle from the lower jaw, and the bony protrusions inside its mouth made it a kind of death trap, similar to the carnivorous (meaning *meat-eating*) Venus flytrap.

It's no wonder the discoverers of *Gerrothorax* called it "the ugliest animal in history." Then again, there are many other contenders for that title.

ICHTYOSAURUS

Mesozoic Era · Jurassic

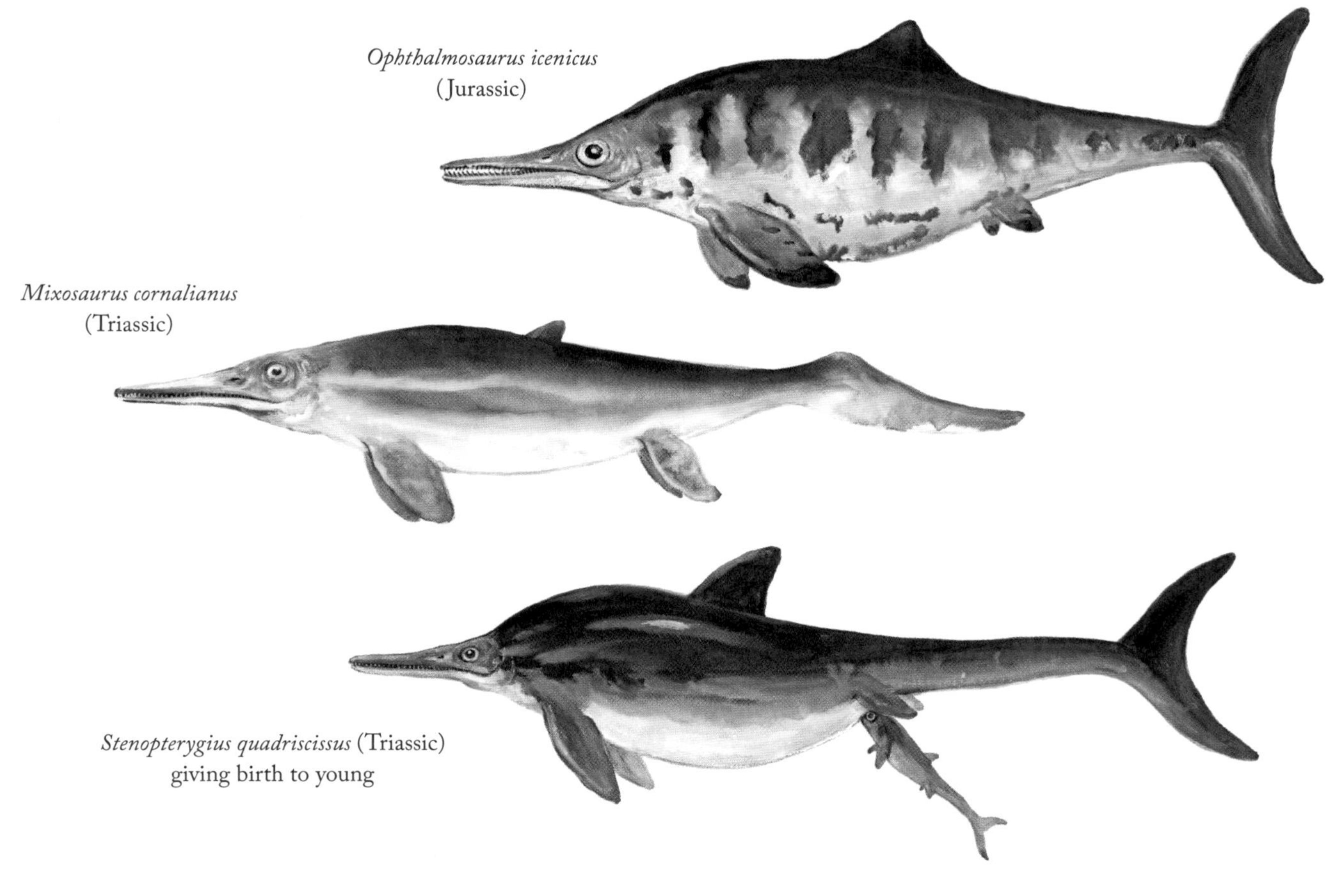

Ophthalmosaurus icenicus (Jurassic)

Mixosaurus cornalianus (Triassic)

Stenopterygius quadriscissus (Triassic) giving birth to young

LENGTH: *Up to 85 feet*
WEIGHT: *Up to 1 ton*

Other than pterosaurs and dinosaurs, ichthyosaurs are the best-known animals of the prehistoric world. Ichthyosaurs were ancient marine reptiles that lived around 240 million years ago. They were a diverse group that separated from terrestrial reptiles and ruled the oceans until about 90 million years ago. Let's take a closer look.

The ichthyosaur, which means "fish lizard," adapted quickly to a watery environment. Some ichthyosaurs had bodies shaped like dolphins and fish, though they are very different from these animals. Some ichthyosaurs were giants like whales, with the largest one ever found (in 2018) being 86 feet long. Fish lizards breathed oxygen from the air and had four fins and big eye sockets. They were great swimmers, able to reach stunning speeds of up to 25 miles per hour.

Ichthyosaur fossils have been discovered all over the world, dating all the way back to 1699. In 1811, the first complete ichthyosaur skeleton was found by 12-year-old Mary Anning, an amateur British fossil collector. This is one of the best-preserved fossil discoveries of the 19th century. Scientists now know that these creatures looked different than originally thought, and recent research on *Stenopterygius* shows it to be warm-blooded with the ability to store fat, like today's cetaceans. *Ichthyosaurs* were a very diverse group with many genera, including the well-known *Ichthyosaurus*. Finds of this species have been recorded in Belgium, the UK, Switzerland, and Germany. It was about six feet long, had a dorsal fin and tail fin, and was a predator with great sight and hearing. It mainly ate fish, mollusks, and cephalopods. Contrary to earlier thinking, fossil evidence has shown that ichthyosaurs were *viviparous*, meaning they gave birth tail-first to prevent drowning.

Ophthalmosaurus, another of the fish lizards, was viviparous too. It was about 16 feet long and had eyes as big as footballs. Its name translates as "Eye lizard."

DIMORPHODON MACRONYX

Mesozoic Era · Jurassic

Pterodactylus kochi
(Jurassic)

Rhamphorhynchus muensteri
(Jurassic)

Anurognathus ammoni
(Jurassic)

WING SPAN: *4.5 feet*
WEIGHT: *4.5 pounds*

Pterosaurs are a famous type of reptile often confused with dinosaurs. Although they come from a different branch of evolution than the dinosaurs, they met the same fate. Among them were some amazing creatures whose skeletons may have inspired the mythical dragon. *Dimorphodon*, a pterosaur found in Europe, is one of the oldest species known.

Pterosaurs were the earliest vertebrates on Earth, and they could fly. They lived during the same time period as dinosaurs, from the Middle Triassic (245 million years ago) to the end of the Cretaceous (66 million years ago). Their wings were leathery membranes that stretched from the body to the front limbs, which had a longer fourth finger. Over 120 genera of pterosaurs have been discovered, and fossils have been found on all continents, even Antarctica. The smallest pterosaurs had a wingspan of only 10 inches, while the largest had a wingspan of over 80 feet, making them the biggest flying creatures ever to have lived on Earth. Like dinosaurs, they were probably warm-blooded, but were replaced by birds at the end of the Cretaceous Period. Birds still exist today.

In December 1828, Mary Anning, a paleontologist, discovered the first fossil remains of *Dimorphodon* in Dorset on the southern coast of England. This area, called the Jurassic Coast, is still a renowned spot for prehistoric fossil discoveries and was the first natural monument in England to be included in the UNESCO World Heritage list. Initially, the fossil finds were placed in the genus *Pterodactylus*. However, in 1858, Richard Owen, a celebrated paleontologist, found additional specimens.

Owen's description led to the discovery of a new reptile genus called *Dimorphodon*, meaning "two-form tooth" due to the rare presence of two types of teeth. This new information changed what was previously known about this animal.

Dimorphodon had a wingspan of nearly five feet. It had an exceptionally long tail and the front of its skull resembled a parrot's beak. Numerous openings over its body, especially on the skull, helped to reduce its weight. Its skull resembled a complex arched bridge, with fang-like teeth in the front of the upper jaw and smaller, flatter teeth behind them and on the lower jaw. At first, *Dimorphodon* was thought to be an *insectivore* (an animal that eats mainly insects), but scientists later speculated it mostly ate fish. Now, due to its movements and flying ability, it is believed that its main diet consisted of small animals with backbones.

It may surprise you to learn that *Dimorphodon* was probably not a great flier. It moved around trees like a squirrel, swooping down on its food in quick, sudden dives. Taking off from the ground was probably a challenge, similar to the way a pheasant does this today.

ARCHAEOPTERYX LITHOGRAPHICA

Mesozoic Era · Jurassic

head and cranium

a fossil found 1887 in Eichstätt, Bavaria
originally described as *Archeornis sicmensi*

WINGSPAN: *2.3 feet*
WEIGHT: *1–2 pounds*

Archaeopteryx is one of the most famous fossils ever discovered. It's mysterious whether this creature was a dinosaur or a bird, and even whether it could fly. An interesting question is: What color were *Archaeopteryx's* feathers?

This ancient creature, known as the "Ancient Wing," is the most well-known prehistoric bird-like creature in the evolutionary chain between dinosaurs and birds. It lived in coastal rainforests in what is now southern Germany, about 148–151 million years ago. It was similar in size to a modern-day crow or pigeon. It had feathers covering its entire body, but it is thought to have been unable to fly actively. It likely used its claws to climb trees and then glided down, using its tail for steering.

The *Archaeopteryx* had a long mouth full of teeth, suggesting it ate insects, crustaceans, and possibly small mammals. It is divided into several species, with the most famous being the *Archaeopteryx lithographica*. We are fortunate to have one of the most famous fossil discoveries of this species.

This find is an imprint of a single feather. It was discovered in the 1850s in a quarry near Solnhofen in the region of Bavaria in Germany. Its description in 1861 caused a scientific stir. Just two years prior, Charles Darwin had published *On the Origin of Species*, introducing his groundbreaking theory of evolution. *Archaeopteryx* had features of both reptiles and birds, making it a potential missing link between the two classes. After comparing *Archaeopteryx* to similar fossils from China, scientists concluded that it was closer to dinosaurs than to birds and that its extinction likely resulted in an evolutionary dead end.

Perhaps, then, things are not quite as they seem. Experts say *Archaeopteryx* may not have even been able to glide, and its wings may have been used instead for hunting or swatting down bugs in flight. There's also a theory that *Archaeopteryx* gradually lost its flying ability, like some birds on islands without predators. Scientists have disproved that *Archaeopteryx* had dark feathers with a green sheen, like in older pictures. In 2020, using modern technology, researchers found that *Archaeopteryx* feathers were light with dark stripes. This means the museum models now need to be redone – but such is our knowledge of evolution, which itself is constantly evolving.

At least ten sets of *Archaeopteryx* bones have been found around the world. Some of these have been sold for huge amounts of money, so they are in private collections. But scientists need to study, explain, and confirm the finds before they can be considered reliable. It looks like there is still a lot to learn about this creature.

MICRORAPTOR GUI

Mesozoic Era · Cretaceous

Sharovipteryx mirabilis
(Triassic)

Acheroraptor temertyorum
(Cretaceous)

Sinosauropteryx prima
(Cretaceous)

WINGSPAN: *3–4 feet*
WEIGHT: *1–3 pounds*

Paleontology is a fascinating science. It demands a basic understanding of biology, as well as an understanding of other fields of study – and a ton of creativity. The story of a feathered dinosaur from the genus *Microraptor* illustrates how difficult it is to accurately determine certain facts. In this case, it is the fundamental question of the origin of birds and their apparent flying ability.

Ever since Charles Darwin's theory of evolution was made public, scientists have been puzzled by the concept of the "flying dinosaur." Then in the late 20th century, evidence of small, winged, and feathered creatures was found in China. It's important to remember that wings have developed independently in various animal groups, such as insects, pterosaurs, dinosaurs, and mammals, and they weren't always used for flying. Nor can it be said for sure that only upper limbs transform into wings. Nowadays, we think of wings as something that helps with flight, but could they have once been used for body warmth and for camouflage? Maybe wings and feathers for flying evolved randomly in a certain group of dinosaurs, which started a successful branch of evolution that led to birds.

Microraptor, meaning "small thief," was a genus of small, feathered dinosaurs that were abundant in what is now northeastern China during the Early Cretaceous Period. We divide *Microraptor* into three species: *Microraptor zhaoianus* (discovered in 2000), *Microraptor gui* (discovered in 2003), and *Microraptor hanqingi* (discovered in 2012). It was about three feet long and weighed a little more than two pounds. The first fossil discovery of this creature became part of a famous hoax known as the *Archaeoraptor*, which was said to be the missing link between dinosaurs and birds, but was actually made up of fossils from multiple animals. After *Archaeoraptor* was featured in National Geographic, its exposure as a fake caused an uproar in the paleontology community.

The discovery of a well-preserved *Microraptor gui* fossil caused great excitement. Its features showed it had wings with feathers on both its front and back legs, plus a mighty feathered tail. People thought it used them to sail among the trees, like a paper kite, while hunting for food like insects, small reptiles, and small mammals. In 2005, however, a new idea came out that changed what people thought. Because of its body and the feathers on its back legs, scientists realized that it could fly like a biplane, with two sets of wings held underneath its body. This meant that birds with the power to fly likely evolved in trees, as most experts previously believed.

Research on this type of creature continues to reveal amazing discoveries. We now think that the *Microraptor* shed its feathers like modern birds do, and its feathers were a gorgeous, shiny black. Not only did its feathers and tail help it fly, but they were also used to communicate with its own kind, especially during mating season – just like modern birds do.

OCULUDENTAVIS KHAUNGRAAE

Mesozoic Era · Cretaceous

a fossil discovered
in a small piece of amber

reconstruction of the simulation
that led to the preservation of the fossil

SKULL LENGTH: *Half an inch*
WEIGHT: *2 g*

When we hear the word "dinosaur," we usually imagine a gigantic beast. But the world of extinct dinosaurs is much more varied than many people think. It's definitely an exciting world, for both beginners and experts. In spring 2020, for example, scientists discovered a new species of dinosaur – only a few inches long! But can that be right?

Even the way in which the alleged smallest dinosaur in the world was discovered is unique. In 2016, a Burmese amber collector named Khaung Ra found a fossilized head with a beak in an amber quarry in Myanmar. The creature was named after its discoverer, in recognition of her contribution to science.

A team of scientists recently discovered a new genus of bird called *Oculudentavis*, which means "eye-toothed bird." It was described in the prestigious magazine *Nature* in the spring of 2020 as another of the many intermediate stages between dinosaur and bird.

The most remarkable thing about this newly discovered dinosaur was its size; it was only a little bigger than today's smallest bird, the bee hummingbird. Its skull was about half an inch long, and scientists estimated that its entire body was only around 0.3 feet long. Its long jaws contained forty small teeth, and the most striking feature was its huge, bulging eyes. This description of the creature fit with what was known about the evolution of birds, and news of the smallest-ever dinosaur caused a sensation. Around the same time, another article was published questioning whether the new genus was actually a dinosaur or just a lizard. This theory was supported by a new discovery in the same area, and we now know that *Oculudentavis* was indeed a prehistoric lizard.

The article in *Nature* magazine had to be retracted, leaving the record for the smallest dinosaur with its current holder. However, this title is likely to change soon. The bee hummingbird is the smallest dinosaur, as birds are now classified as dinosaurs, because they are the direct descendants of them. Among "non-avian" dinosaurs, *Anchiornis huxleyi* is a strong contender for the smallest creature. Found in China in 2009, it was about the size of a sparrow.

The discoveries of fossils in amber in Myanmar have raised ethical concerns. In a country that has experienced civil war for a long time, these finds could easily be exploited for illegal and immoral business purposes, and this might even already be happening. Even though some of these finds, such as a feathered dinosaur's tail, are truly remarkable, some leading paleontologists are asking people to stop studying these fossils until there is a ceasefire in Myanmar.

ARGENTINOSAURUS HUINCULENSIS

Mesozoic Era · Cretaceous

Argentinosaurus huinculensis (Cretaceous)

Brontosaurus excelsus (Jurassic) an idea from the late 18th century to the early 20th century

Brontosaurus excelsus (Jurassic) current idea

LENGTH: *100–115 feet*
WEIGHT: *60–75 tons*

When people think of dinosaurs, they usually imagine huge creatures. However, some dinosaur species were surprisingly small. Which was the biggest of them all? Recent research suggests it was *Argentinosaurus*, which means "Argentinian lizard." This long-necked reptile is likely the largest land animal that has ever lived on Earth.

The home of *Argentinosaurus* was Patagonia, in southern Argentina. In 1987, its fossils were discovered, and scientists learned more about it six years later. Although no complete skeleton has been found, the large vertebrae that were discovered (which were over five feet long) give us a good idea of its size. We think that *Argentinosaurus huinculensis* was nearly 120 feet long, a length surpassed in today's animal kingdom only by blue whales.

Argentinosaurus was a herbivorous (meaning *plant-eating*) dinosaur that could travel at about five miles per hour. Scientists think it made up to 880 pounds of poop every day! Experts don't agree on how much it weighed, but it was probably between 75 tons and 95 tons. That's heavier than a jet airplane! But, according to experts in biomechanics, a land animal can theoretically weigh up to 130 tons, although such an animal would be unable to move. For cetaceans, like the blue whale, the water helps them to stay afloat, so they can weigh almost 200 tons.

It's hard to figure out how big *Argentinosaurus* was because we only have about 10 percent of its skeleton. We do know that one of its thigh bones was eight feet long and its heart weighed over 440 pounds. We don't know why *Argentinosaurus* and its relatives got so huge, but it could have been a mix of things like having lots of available food, a warm climate, and the fact that the great weight of the skeleton of large dinosaurs was relieved by air pockets in the body, as is the case with birds.

As if all this were not enough, some people believe that even bigger dinosaurs may have lived in the same area as *Argentinosaurus*. Some of these theories are pretty wild. For example, is this a giant bone? Or a petrified tree trunk?

ELASMOSAURUS PLATYURUS

Mesozoic Era · Cretaceous

Morturneria seymourensis
(Cretaceous)

Plesiosaurus dolichodeirus
(Cretaceous)

Elasmosaurus platyurus
(Cretaceous)

LENGTH: *33 feet*
WEIGHT: *2 tons*

You've probably heard of the Loch Ness Monster, an enormous reptile said to live in Scotland's Loch Ness lake. Its long neck reminds us of the prehistoric rulers of the oceans, plesiosaurs. Plesiosaurs lived during the Mesozoic era, during the same time as the dinosaurs, but they weren't dinosaurs and the two orders weren't related. Plesiosaurs first appeared 203 million years ago and lived until the end of the era of the great reptiles, 66 million years ago.

Enormous predators at the top of the food chain, they had four flippers and a long neck. They were excellent swimmers, inhabiting all parts of the world's oceans. Some of them grew to be 66 feet long, although most were much smaller. The first fossil of the species *Plesiosaurus dolichodeirus* was found in 1821 by Mary Anning, an amateur paleontologist who had earlier discovered the *Ichthyosaurus*. *Elasmosaurus*, a representative of the plesiosaurs, is characterized by its long neck. It inhabited the seas around the territory of North America. Although it was scientifically described as early as 1868, the reconstruction of the creature's skeleton made by this describer was wrong; indeed, he placed *Elasmosaurus*'s skull at the end of its tail. It was up to 46 feet long, most of which was accounted for by its extremely long neck. We are now able to distinguish eight *Elasmosaurus* species. A predator, it fed mainly on fish and ammonites. It made good use of its long, supple neck when pouncing on its prey.

Recent discoveries have revealed that not all plesiosaurs were predators. In Antarctica, a new species of plesiosaur was found and named *Morturneria*. This species was part of the youngest branch of evolution, and its remarkable teeth were long, narrow, delicate, and pointed outward, resembling the trap of a carnivorous plant. *Morturneria* likely fed on small aquatic crustaceans, like cetaceans do today, showing evidence of convergent evolution, which is when different animals evolve similar things separately.

Although long extinct, plesiosaurs still fascinate us. In 2009, a team of American scientists created an underwater robot that moves like plesiosaurs did, using its tail like most aquatic creatures, but also its flippers, which act as paddles. This robot was modeled after the extinct species *Quetzalcoatlus northropi*, which lived during the Mesozoic and Cretaceous Periods.

QUETZALCOATLUS NORTHROPI

Mesozoic Era · Cretaceous

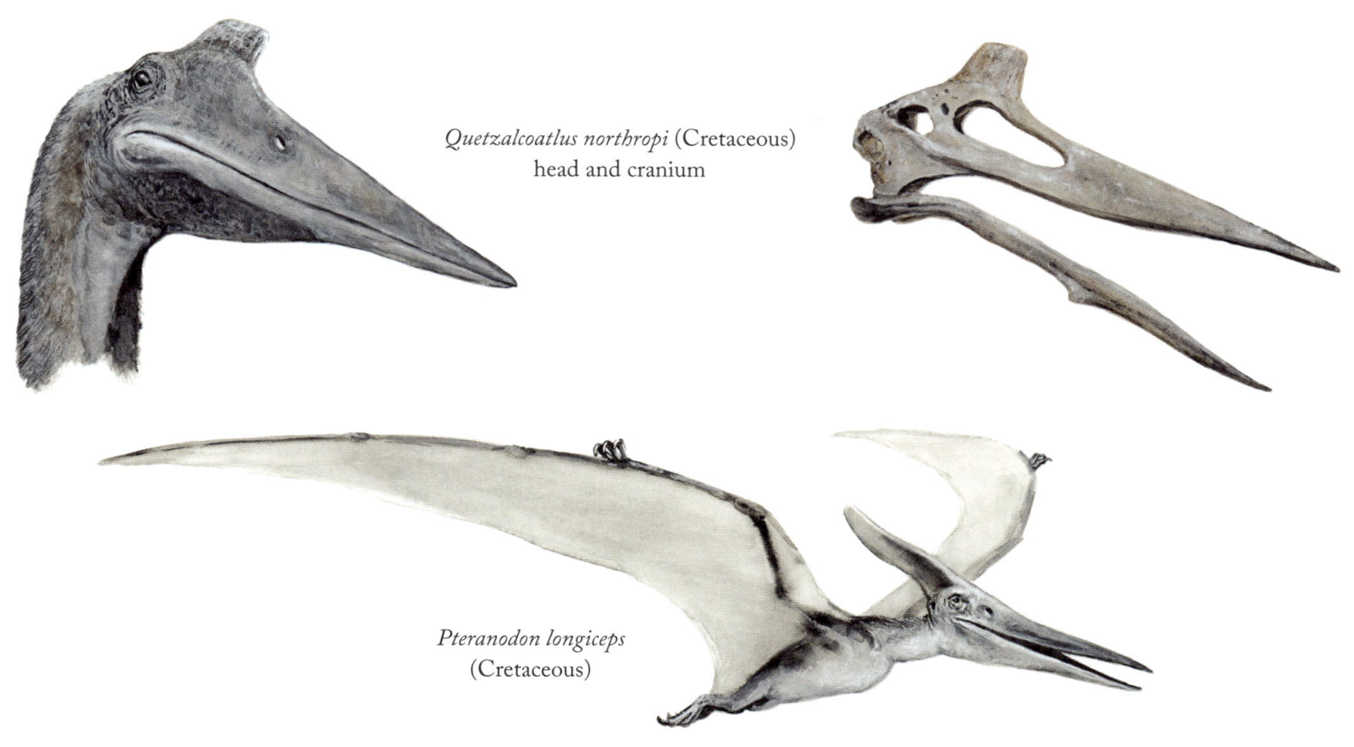

Quetzalcoatlus northropi (Cretaceous) head and cranium

Pteranodon longiceps (Cretaceous)

WINGSPAN: *Up to 40 feet*
WEIGHT: *550 pounds*

Not all pterosaurs were as clumsy in the air as *Dimorphodon*. Far from it – some could fly with the skill and grace of an airplane pilot. *Quetzalcoatlus* was one of the biggest flying creatures ever. Its flying abilities still puzzle biologists and engineers. *Quetzalcoatlus* was named after an Aztec feathered serpent god. It ruled the skies of North America in the Late Cretaceous Period, making it one of the last giant reptile species. The first fossils of *Quetzalcoatlus* were found in what is now Texas. Scientists estimate it had a wingspan of nearly 40 feet, similar to that of a small airliner. Amazingly, it only weighed about 550 pounds – if it had been any heavier, it wouldn't have been able to fly.

It had a shockingly long neck and an enormous, stretched-out head, which, together with its toothless beak, added up to a length of eight feet. Opinions vary on what *Quetzalcoatlus* ate. One theory is that it was a fish-eater, and its job in the environment was similar to that of the modern-day wandering albatross (the bird with the longest wingspan).

Quetzalcoatlus bones have been found deep inland, leading to the theory that it was a scavenger gliding for hours above the plains in search of dinosaur carrion. Its long neck could have been used to reach the insides of large carcasses. The latest hypothesis, though, suggests that *Quetzalcoatlus* walked the landscape, like a stork, eating whatever it could find, such as baby animals. In any case, you may be wondering how an animal tall enough to look a giraffe in the eye could take off from the ground. Various biomechanical theories explain its ability to fly, such as the idea that it needed a cliff above open sea to take off. However, there were no cliffs in the area when it lived. Most scientists believe *Quetzalcoatlus* got into the air by using all four powerful limbs in a leap, like a catapult.

Computer animation gives us another perspective: it shows us that *Quetzalcoatlus*'s take-off was similar to that of a hang-glider. To gain enough speed to fly, this huge pterosaur would have run down a hill on all fours into the wind. Because of its light, delicate bones, it had to be very careful when landing. Recently, it was discovered that pterosaurs were covered with hair-like fibers called pycnofibers. We have also recently learned that the *Pterandon*, which lived in what is now America and had a wingspan of over 20 feet, could change the air pressure in its hollow bones. The pterosaur kingdom will surely continue to surprise us, not only because of its members' flying abilities.

ARCHELON ISCHYROS

Mesozoic Era · Cretaceous

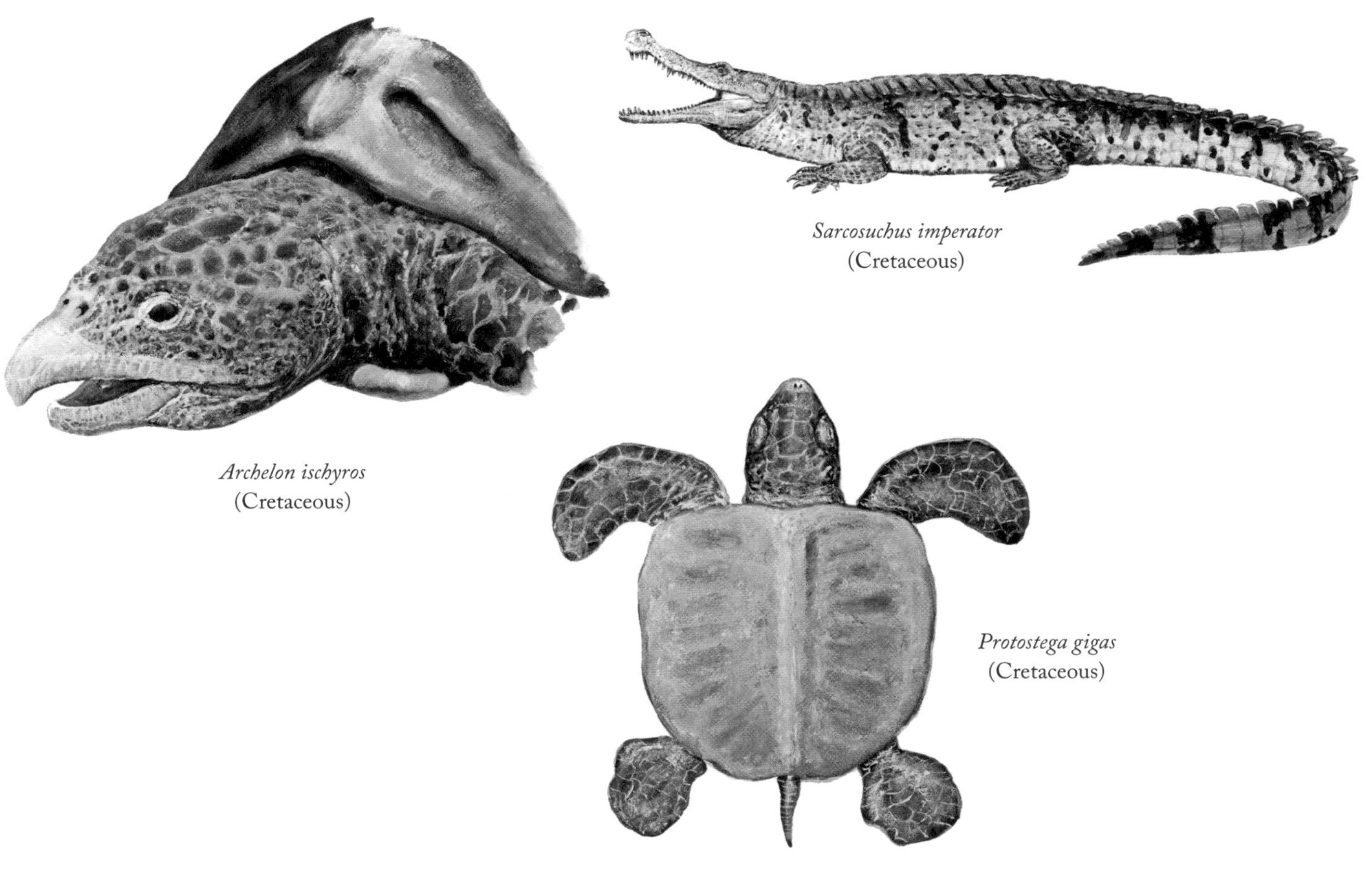

Sarcosuchus imperator (Cretaceous)

Archelon ischyros (Cretaceous)

Protostega gigas (Cretaceous)

LENGTH: *15 feet*
WEIGHT: *Over 2 tons*

The Mesozoic Era is often thought of as the Age of Dinosaurs, but many other huge creatures lived during this time that were not dinosaurs. One of them was *Archelon*, which means "ruling turtle." This animal was much bigger than the turtles we know today.

Turtles have been around since at least 220 million years ago! *Archelon*, the largest turtle ever discovered, lived during the time of the last dinosaurs. In 1895, the first *Archelon* fossil was found in South Dakota. The following year, a paleontologist named G. R. Wieland named and described it. *Archelon* swam in what was then the Western Interior Seaway, feasting on marine organisms and aquatic plants. The biggest *Archelon* ever discovered was a whopping 15 feet long and almost 16 feet wide. It's estimated to have weighed over two tons!

Archelon is an ancient ancestor of the leatherback sea turtle, which can grow to be quite large. Instead of a hard shell, it had a leathery membrane or a thin layer of bone, so it couldn't hide from predators like sharks or large reptiles the way turtles can. It ate with its hooked beak, which also served as a defense. We think *Archelon* reproduced like modern sea turtles, laying eggs on the shore once a year. It is believed that these turtles, like modern ones, could live for over 100 years.

Another long-lived animal of the Mesozoic Era is the *Sarcosuchus imperator*, or the "SuperCroc," a giant reptile that lived in the rivers of North Africa and possibly South America 115 million years ago – long before *Archelon*. This distant cousin of the crocodile was a whopping 39 feet long and weighed up to 22,000 pounds – about the same size as some of its dinosaur contemporaries. It likely hunted dinosaurs, but mostly would have eaten fish and smaller animals.

Not only animals have changed over time: Earth's deserts, forests, and even entire continents were very different in the deep past. Changes in the environment have always been shaped by geological processes. Humans have made huge changes to the land in a very short period of time, like no other creature. Unfortunately, this change is not always positive.

TYRANNOSAURUS REX

Mesozoic Era · Cretaceous

cranium

LENGTH: *40 feet*
WEIGHT: *9.5 tons*

Some prehistoric animals are so well known that one could easily believe that we know everything about them. This is far from true, however. Even the much-studied dinosaur *Tyrannosaurus rex*, which was formally described as early as 1905, keeps providing us with new, unexpected facts.

Until the 1990s, *Tyrannosaurus rex* (meaning "tyrannical king lizard") was thought to be the biggest carnivorous dinosaur and the biggest land predator of all time. It's no longer the record-holder, although it still holds the title of the heaviest known land predator of all time. The most famous and best-preserved *T. rex* skeleton is named Sue, after its discoverer, and is on display at a museum in Chicago. Sue is 40 feet long and nearly 10 tons, although other *T. rexes* were typically two tons lighter. With their excellent sense of smell and sight, tyrannosaurids hunted small dinosaurs, crushing them with the strongest jaws ever seen on land.

We still don't know how fast *Tyrannosaurus rex* could move. At first, it was thought it could chase its prey quickly. Studies said it could go up to 40 miles per hour, faster than the fastest human runners. Later, it was thought it could reach only 25 mph. But now, scientists think that because of its heavy body, it couldn't run. It probably walked quickly and could go a long distance.

Scientists have been able to answer questions about *Tyrannosaurus rex*'s physical appearance. We know that, unlike earlier tyrannosaurids, they had no feathers. It seems they lost their feathers due to their size and environment, much like elephants, as a species, lost their fur long ago. We still don't know what the purpose of *T. rex*'s tiny arms were. They were about the size of an adult human's arms, but much stronger. *T. rex* couldn't even reach its mouth with these limbs, nor could these limbs touch each other. Yet they must have had a purpose – and there are a few theories. Maybe it used them to grab its prey, for example. Or perhaps it used them to push off the ground. Maybe the limbs had long claws, and so could be used as weapons.

Tyrannosaurids were some of the last dinosaurs to exist. They were very likely alive when the Earth was hit by the asteroid Chicxulub. Around 6–9 miles in diameter, this asteroid struck Earth 66 million years ago on what is now Mexico's Yucatán Peninsula and killed off all the dinosaurs (not counting the smaller ones, which later evolved into modern-day birds).

ANKYLOSAURUS MAGNIVENTRIS

Mesozoic Era · Cretaceous

protection from tyrannosaurus

tail detail

Sauropelta edwardsoni
(Cretaceous)

LENGTH: *26–30 feet*
WEIGHT: *8 tons*

Prehistoric reptiles were incredibly successful animals, mastering water, air, and land. Some herbivorous (strictly plant-eating) dinosaurs even became "walking fortresses" that no predator dared challenge, like *Ankylosaurus magniventris* – the largest and youngest species of ankylosaurids. When *Ankylosaurus* fossils were first discovered in Montana in the early 20th century, scientists thought it was a predator. Later, it was determined to be a herbivore with body armor and a large, mobile tail club. Its armor was made of large plates of bone, mainly on the upper body. Recent research suggests that *Ankylosaurus* was between 26 and 29 feet long and weighed about eight tons.

Ankylosaurus – its name loosely means "fused lizard" – lived until the end of the dinosaur era, right around 66 million years ago. It shared the same habitat as *Tyrannosaurus rex*, the plains of North America, so it's likely they ran into each other.

Ankylosaurus, equipped with a formidable tail club for self-defense, lived in areas of higher elevation, where it would forage for low-lying vegetation, shielded by its sturdy bony plates. In contrast, the nodosaurid species *Sauropelta edwardsorum*, measuring approximately 16 feet in length and weighing around 3,300 pounds, boasted large spikes protruding from their necks and backs. These spikes served as additional defense mechanisms, offering protection against potential predators.

TITANOBOA CERREJONENSIS

Cenozoic Era · paleogén – Eocene

Carbonemys cofrinii (Paleocene)
hypotetical reconstruction of appearance

Puentemys mushaisaensis (Paleocene)
hypotetical reconstruction of appearance

LENGTH: *42 feet*
WEIGHT: *1.1 tons*

Scientists long believed that the biggest prehistoric snake was *Gigantophis*, which lived in Egypt about 40 million years ago. But even bigger was *Titanoboa*, a giant snake from the Boidae family that lived 20 million years earlier, on another continent.

In 2009, an international expedition led by paleontologist Jonathan Bloch from the University of Florida explored the Cerrejón coal mine in northeastern Colombia. To their surprise, they discovered an almost complete spine and 184 other bones from 28 giant snake specimens. The snake genus was named *Titanoboa*, after the modern boa constrictor snake and the Titans of Ancient Greek mythology. With the largest snake vertebrae ever discovered, they were able to accurately reconstruct the animal's size. *Titanoboa* was about 42 feet long and well over 2 tons – making it one of the biggest predators on land since the dinosaurs went extinct.

Titanoboa proved to be the longest snake ever discovered. It was nine feet longer than its ancient relative from North Africa, and nearly twice as long as the largest snake of today, South America's green anaconda! Even so, *Titanoboa* and the anaconda are related. This begs the question of why modern anacondas don't reach such impressive sizes. The answer is that snakes are warm-blooded animals, and their size depends on the temperature of their environment. The size of *Titanoboa* suggests that it lived in an area with an average annual temperature of 86–95°F, much higher than was previously known.

At first, it was thought that *Titanoboa* lived like an anaconda. But studying its jaw and the climate of the time showed that it lived mostly in water. Its sharp teeth suggest it ate mostly fish and maybe even crocodiles. Its huge body made it float easily in rivers and shallow pools, which made it easier to move around. In the relatively young ecosystem of tropical primeval forests, it rained twice as much as it does today.

At the same mines, other surprising discoveries were made. Scientists discovered ancient species of turtles that had developed different tactics to protect themselves from giant predators. *Puentemys mushaisaensis* had an "unswallowable" shell that was five feet in diameter. *Cerrejonemys wayuunaiki* had an "unbitable" shell that was 1.5 inches thick. As for the "coal turtle" *Carbonemys*, it seems that like *Titanoboa*, it could take on a crocodile!

EOHIPPUS ANGUSTIDENS

Cenozoic Era · Eocene

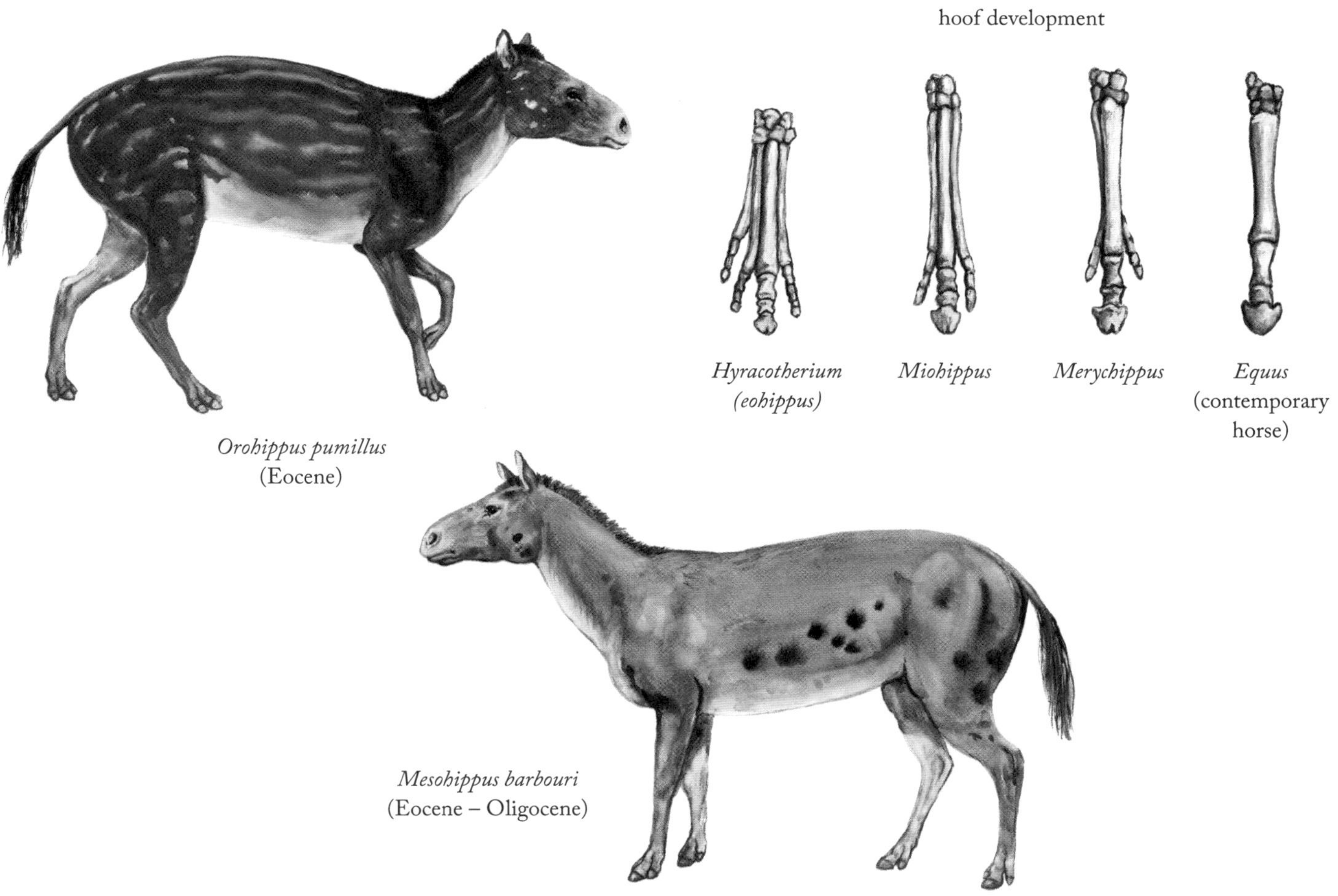

Orohippus pumillus (Eocene)

Mesohippus barbouri (Eocene – Oligocene)

HEIGHT: *12–24 inches*
WEIGHT: *7–77 pounds*

When we think of horses, we see strong, swift animals closely connected, emotionally, to humans. Before being domesticated, though, horses were wild creatures. Their evolution began with *Eohippus*, which was about the size of a fox. This herbivore looked more like a young tapir than a horse, with a small head, eyes at the front, and a light, slender body. Its legs were short, with four toes on the front feet and three on the hinds. These toes were protected by small hooves. It placed its weight on the pads behind them, and its coat may have resembled that of a fallow deer, with spots or stripes on a dark background. This is likely because it lived in swampy forests, where such coloring is common.

In 1841, a fossil was discovered in England by celebrated paleontologist Richard Owen. The shape of its teeth led Owen to think that these were the remains of a primate, which he later specified as a hyrax, a small furry mammal from which it gets its Latin name *Hyracotherium*, meaning "like a hyrax." In 1876, an almost complete skeleton was found in Wyoming and was named *Eohippus*, which means "dawn horse" (Eos is the Greek goddess of the dawn). It was later determined that these two species were the same, which explains why both names are still used. This is because when the early equid lived, Europe and North America were connected by a land bridge, so it evolved to become different species as the ecosystem changed. It adapted to the steppe by becoming larger, faster, and more agile to survive. The hardness of the soil caused the horse to develop hooves – hard coverings on the feet to protect the middle toe. Recent research suggests that *Eohippus* may not be a direct ancestor of the modern horse, but it still belongs to the Equidae family.

UINTATHERIUM ANCEPS

Cenozoic Era · Eocene

Gobiatherium major
(Eocene)

Megacerops platyceras (brontotherium)
(Oligocene)

Arsinoitherium zitteli
(Oligocene)

HEIGHT: *5.6 feet*
WEIGHT: *Over 2 tons*

This animal was possibly the largest mammal of its time and probably the first to weigh over a ton. Its skull had a unique, downright bizarre shape, so it's no wonder *Uintatherium* is such a beloved prehistoric creature. Its fossil history is fascinating too.

At first glance, *Uintatherium* may remind you of today's rhinoceros, due to its large size. We think it was around 13 feet long, over five feet tall, and over two tons in weight. Its most notable feature is its huge skull, which was about three feet long and had bone outgrowths (*ossicones*) that looked like the horns on a giraffe's skull. Scientists are still debating what the purpose of these "horns" were; since they are bigger on males, they probably were used in fights between males and females.

The upper jaw of *Uintatherium* had huge, eight-inch-long teeth that resembled those of the saber-toothed tiger. But these teeth weren't dangerous; *Uintatherium* probably used them to pluck aquatic plants from the marshes to eat. Initially, only one species of *Uintatherium* living in North America was known and described, called *Uintatherium anceps*. In the early 1980s, a *Uintatherium* skull was discovered in China, which was very surprising. This led to the description of *Uintatherium insperatus*, which was a bit younger than *U. anceps* in terms of evolution.

In 1870, the first fossils were discovered in Wyoming, sparking the so-called "Bone Wars" between two paleontologists, Othniel Charles Marsh and Edward Drinker Cope. The two competed fiercely for who could discover and describe more extinct species, even going so far as to slander and scheme against each other. Looking back, their work resulted in a huge increase in interest in paleontology and the description of over 100 dinosaur species.

But how did *Uintatherium* come by its strange name? The answer is simple: it comes from the place it was found, the Uinta Mountains, with its name meaning "beast of the Uinta Mountains."

ANDREWSARCHUS MONGOLIENSIS

Cenozoic Era · Eocene

head and cranium

Sinonyx jiashanensis
(Paleocene)

HEIGHT: *6.5 feet*
WEIGHT: *Over 2 tons*

For mammals to evolve into the countless shapes and sizes we see today, living in different environments and eating all kinds of different food, it took hundreds of millions of years. *Andrewsarchus* was one of the first mammals. All we know about it is from one skull that was found. Even so, scientists have attempted to describe and reconstruct it.

Andrewsarchus likely resembled today's wolves and hyenas. It likely lived a similar lifestyle, potentially as a feared predator and scavenger. Surprisingly, *Andrewsarchus* was not a beast of prey but an ancient ungulate. It may have been omnivorous, with massive jaws and strong teeth that could crush bone and shell. We know for certain that it was one of the largest known predatory land mammals ever. It was probably between 13 and 20 feet long, and may have been almost 6 feet tall. Estimates put its weight at up to 1,300 pounds. Instead of claws, it probably had a small hoof on each of its five toes.

All we know about *Andrewsarchus* comes from the discovery of a single skull and, later, fragments of several bones. The skull is about twice the size as that of a grizzly bear, measuring 33 inches long and 22 inches wide. It was discovered in 1923 in the Gobi Desert of Inner Mongolia by an expedition led by Roy Chapman Andrews, an American paleontologist and adventurer famous for promoting his own work. The adventure movie character Indiana Jones is said to be based on him. The word "archus" in Greek means "ruler." The skull is now a prized artifact in the American Museum of Natural History in New York City. We are still waiting to find a complete skeleton of this animal.

It was once thought that *Andrewsarchus* was the ancestor of modern whales. Today we know this to be the case only through its sister line. It is also possible to trace its lineage to present-day hippos.

PEREGOCETUS PACIFICUS

Cenozoic Era · Eocene

Ambulocetus natans (Eocene)

Indohyus indirae (Eocene)

Pakicetus sp. (Eocene)

LENGTH: *13 feet*
WEIGHT: *Unknown*

The incredible story of the evolution of cetaceans (whales, dolphins, porpoises, and narwhals) is one of the most fascinating tales in all of paleontology. The theory that they evolved from pig-like animals that gradually moved from land to sea may seem unbelievable, but it is likely true. This hypothesis is bolstered by the recent discovery of a species that serves as an important evolutionary link.

The hippopotamus is the closest living relative of the whale, and both species live in the water. It may come as a surprise, but whales did not always live in the ocean – they used to live on land. This is, however, a common occurrence in evolution, and whales are an example of this taken to the extreme. From an ecological point of view, whales replaced the extinct giant marine reptiles. For whales to fully adapt to life in the water, their ancestors had to change a lot. There is a theory that cetaceans (whales, dolphins, porpoises, and narwhals) evolved from primitive predatory ungulates, which had a similar lifestyle to predatory mammals today.

The best-known ancestor of whales is the scary-looking *Andrewsarchus*. Many cetaceans today are predators, but some, like whales, are not. There's a theory that whales evolved from primitive biungulates, which relocated into the water to get away from predators. In 1992, in a desert in Pakistan, they found the remains of a "primitive whale" called *Ambulocetus*. Scientists think it could only hear underwater and lived between 50 and 80 million years ago. In Kashmir, they found a creature called *Indohyus*, which was the size of a cat, between 48 and 55 million years old. It looked like today's pigs and foxes. But they didn't yet have proof that the tail and limbs changed into fins.

This changed in 2019, with the publication of a study based on a discovery made in Peru in 2011. Fossils of a thirteen-foot-long, four-legged creature named *Peregocetus pacificus* were found. It was an amphibious ancestor of cetaceans, and the fossils showed that it had a long tail adapted for swimming. Its teeth suggested its lifestyle was similar to that of an otter. The remains were found off the Pacific coast of South America, suggesting these creatures had swum there from Asia. This indicates favorable sea currents and reinforces that the two continents were once half as far apart as they are today.

Cetaceans, such as whales, dolphins, porpoises, and narwhals, have evolved into a variety of creatures. Unfortunately, due to human activities, many of these species are at risk of disappearing forever. What can be done, then, to help protect them?

ANTHROPORNIS NORDENSKJOELDI

Cenozoic Era · Eocene – Oligocene

Waimanu manneringi
(Paleocene)

Icadyptes salasi
(Eocene)

Crossvallia waiparensis
(Paleocene)

HEIGHT: *6.6 feet*
WEIGHT: *88 pounds*

Everyone knows the cute-looking inhabitant of the South Pole called the penguin. But not everyone knows how intelligent the penguin is, or how long its evolution has been. Penguins are found throughout the Southern Hemisphere. The Galápagos penguin occurs in the Northern Hemisphere too.

Around 70 million years ago, Zealandia separated from Australia, forming New Zealand and some nearby islands. This is where the earliest penguin fossils, of the *Waimanu* genus, were discovered. It had a long, slender beak and long wings. Over time, penguins evolved to become well-suited to life in the water and in cold temperatures.

About 60 million years ago, shortly after the dinosaurs went extinct, penguins were thriving. They explored new areas, adjusted to their surroundings, and changed over time. Evidence of their success is their growth to enormous sizes. About 40 million years ago, the genus *Anthropornis* (which means "man-bird" in Latin) was around 6.5 feet long and weighed around 220 pounds! This growth was likely due to the absence of large marine reptiles to eat them. The pressures of evolution may have caused the eventual extinction of giant penguins, though, as marine mammals began to take their place.

Anthropornis was discovered on Seymour Island off the coast of Antarctica and New Zealand. Polish paleontologist Piotr Jadwiszczak was able to assemble the fossilized remains into a penguin larger than a human. Its huge wings were much bigger compared to its body, which meant it was an amazing swimmer and could dive deeper than the emperor penguin – the deepest-diving penguin today, standing at four feet tall and able to reach impressive depths of a third of a mile!

A study published in 2019 uncovered evidence of a giant penguin species that lived in New Zealand. This species, called *Crossvallia waiparensis*, was twice as big as the kakapo owl parrot, which can still be found in New Zealand today. This giant penguin lived alongside another extinct creature, the *Heracles inexpectatus*, a giant parrot that lived 19 million years ago and was about three feet tall.

BASILOSAURUS CETOIDES

Cenozoic Era · Eocene

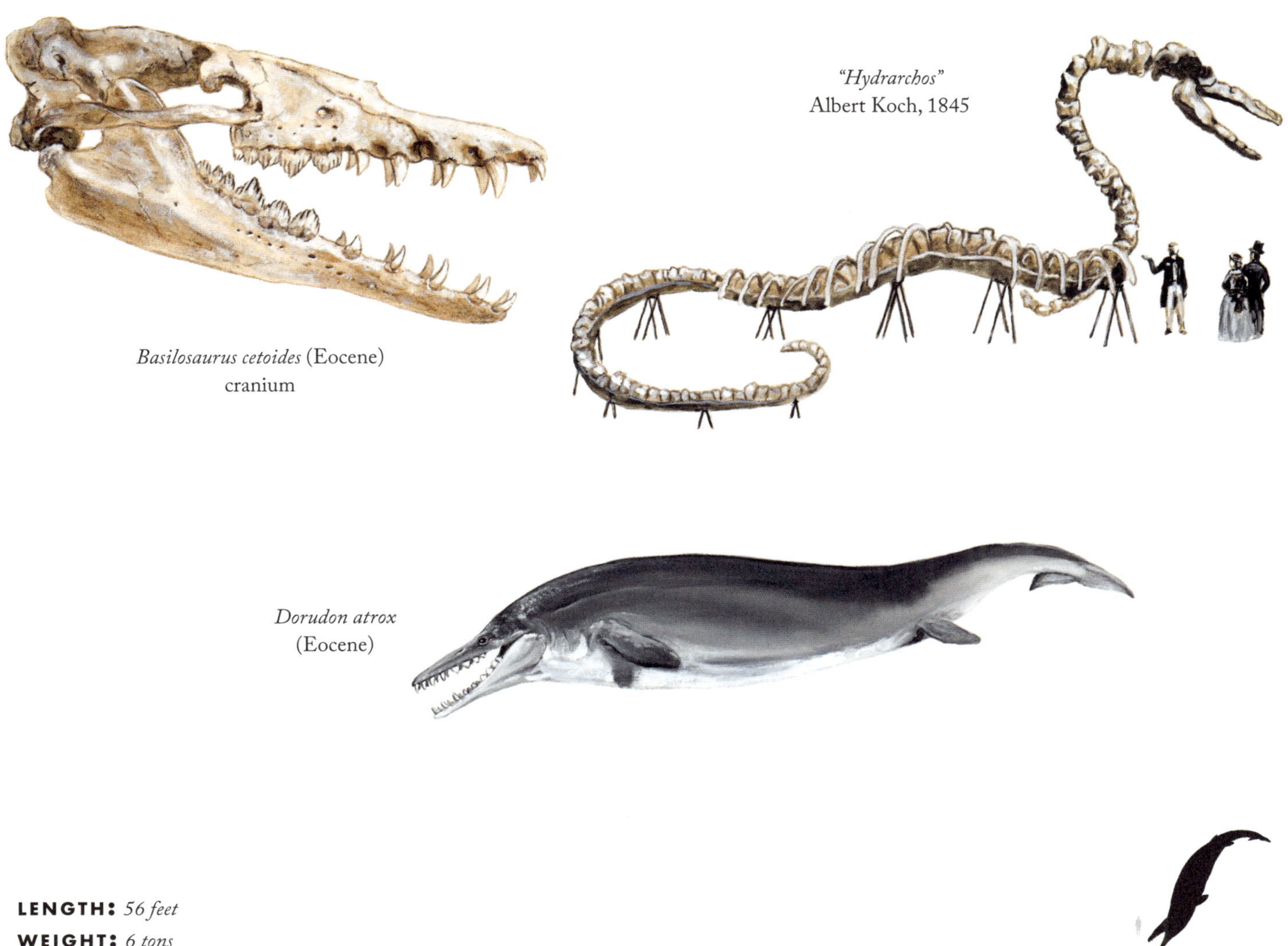

Basilosaurus cetoides (Eocene)
cranium

"Hydrarchos"
Albert Koch, 1845

Dorudon atrox
(Eocene)

LENGTH: *56 feet*
WEIGHT: *6 tons*

Basilosaurus is known as the "King Lizard." Although the scientists who first discovered its fossils mistook it for a long reptile, it's actually an ancestor of modern-day aquatic mammals like the sperm whale. It was about 66 feet long, larger than most sperm whale specimens today. It had fore and hind limbs, but they were reduced. Its front flippers were jointed at the elbow. Its body was slender and snake-like, with a short skull at one end and a fluke (a wide flat tail) at the other, like modern-day cetaceans. The *Basilosaurus* made its body longer by stretching its vertebrae, giving it great flexibility in its spine. An adult probably weighed around 6 tons.

Unlike the nostrils of modern cetaceans, which are on the top of the head, *Basilosaurus* had nostrils located in the middle of its head, between its eyes and mouth. Its mouth was full of 44 teeth of different shapes, including sharp front canines to grab the prey and flat, jagged back teeth to break the food into pieces.

The power of its bite was immense – in today's animal kingdom, only the giant sea reptiles can exert a similar force. Thanks to an incredible discovery in Egypt, we now know what *Basilosaurus* ate – large fish and the young of the small cetacean *Dorudon*. In America, *Basilosaurus* also hunted sharks and fish.

Today, there are two types of these creatures known: *Basilosaurus cetoides*, first discovered in North America, and the smaller *Basilosaurus isis*, found in Egypt. Both lived in the huge ocean that connected the ancient continents. In 1834, *Basilosaurus* was described for the first time from fossils, but incorrectly. A few years later, in 1839, Richard Owen, an English professor of comparative anatomy, proved it was actually a mammal. In 1845, *Hydrarchos*, which was believed to be a sea monster, was put on display in New York. Such an animal never truly existed, though – it was a hoax made up of *Basilosaurus* bones. Albert Koch, the creator of this fake *Hydrarchos* animal, later took it on a successful tour around Europe.

Due to confusion about where the fossils came from, scientists gave this creature the Latin name *Zeuglodon etoides*. This was an attempt by Richard Owen to correct the initial incorrect descriptions of this creature. However, according to the rules of taxonomy, the original name *Basilosaurus* ("King lizard") is the correct name.

ENTELODON MAGNUS

Cenozoic Era · Eocene – Oligocene

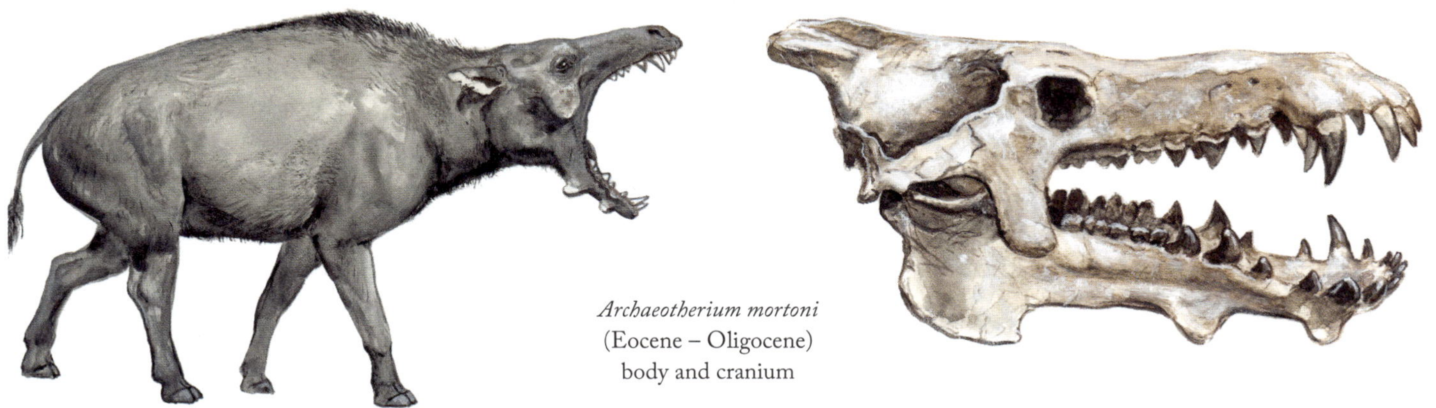

Archaeotherium mortoni
(Eocene – Oligocene)
body and cranium

Daeodon shoshonensis
(Oligocene – Miocene)

HEIGHT: *4.4 feet*
WEIGHT: *330 pounds – 1 ton*

Surprisingly, one of the most-feared mammals of the early Tertiary Period was not a canine or a feline. *Entelodon*, as it was called, looked like an angry pig – and acted like one too! Even though it was an ungulate, it was closely related to whales and hippos. Its body and big skull were perfect for hunting and gathering food. It would even eat carrion. Its strong legs and body enabled it to chase its prey across the plains, where it lived for a very long time. Its most remarkable features were its teeth and jaws: it had incisors for tearing and molars for crushing bones. Its Latin name means "complete set of teeth," and its strong cheekbones and cheek muscles only increased the pressure of its grip.

The *Entelodon* hunted anything, anywhere, including (most likely) the ancestor of the horse, *Eohippus*, and smaller rhinoceroses. Only the biggest carnivores could compete with it. Its ability to eat a variety of food and to survive in different places allowed it to live on Earth for 10 million years. Some of its species even crossed the Bering Strait to North America. Today, we distinguish the *Entelodon* genus in eight species that inhabited a vast area of Eurasia, from modern-day Western Europe to Mongolia and China, perhaps even reaching Japan. This monster weighed about a ton and was over eight feet long, with a third of that being its skull and neck. Its great adaptability allowed it to live in scrubland and swamps.

Fossils of this creature have been known to us for a long time. Initially, it was hard to know what the fossils belonged to, and some people even thought they were from a bear. Eventually, it was determined that the fossils were from an *Entelodon*.

PARACERATHERIUM TRANSOURALICUM

Cenozoic Era · Oligocene – Miocene

Metamynodon planifrons
(Oligocene)

Hyracodon nebraskensis
(Eocene – Oligocene)

Teleoceras proterum
(Miocene – Pliocene)

LENGTH: *Up to 26 feet*
WEIGHT: *15–20 tons*

Paraceratherium is the biggest and heaviest land mammal of all time! It was related to the rhinoceros and was earlier known as *Indricotherium*, *Baluchitherium*, and other names. It was 16 feet tall, which is as tall as a modern giraffe – only it was so bulky it weighed 20 times more than a giraffe!

Scientists still debate exactly how much *Paraceratherium* weighed, but estimates range between 12 and 20 tons! Without its neck and head, it was about 16 feet tall and 16 feet long – much bigger than all elephants except for *Palaeloxon namadicus*, a giant relative of the elephant that could reach a similar weight but didn't appear in Eastern Asia until much later.

Paraceratherium was a long-lived, giant herbivore that developed a long neck for the same reason the giraffe did – to reach the treetops. Instead of having a horn on its skull, it had two cone-shaped, tusk-like upper incisors. It also had a square nostril, suggesting it had a small trunk or prehensile upper lip. It probably ate a lot, which explains why its long legs could cover large distances, as evidenced by the variety of places its fossils have been found.

As early as 1846, *Paraceratherium* fossils were discovered on the territory of today's Pakistan. In 1911, British researchers described and named the creature. Later, US, Chinese, and Soviet research teams found more remains in various places in Southern Eurasia. Since research results weren't shared internationally a century ago, this caused confusion regarding the creature's taxonomy, which is why *Paraceratherium* was previously known by other names. We only know its size from fragments of individual bones, from which only estimates can be drawn.

SIMBAKUBWA KUTOKAAFRIKA

Cenozoic Era · Miocene

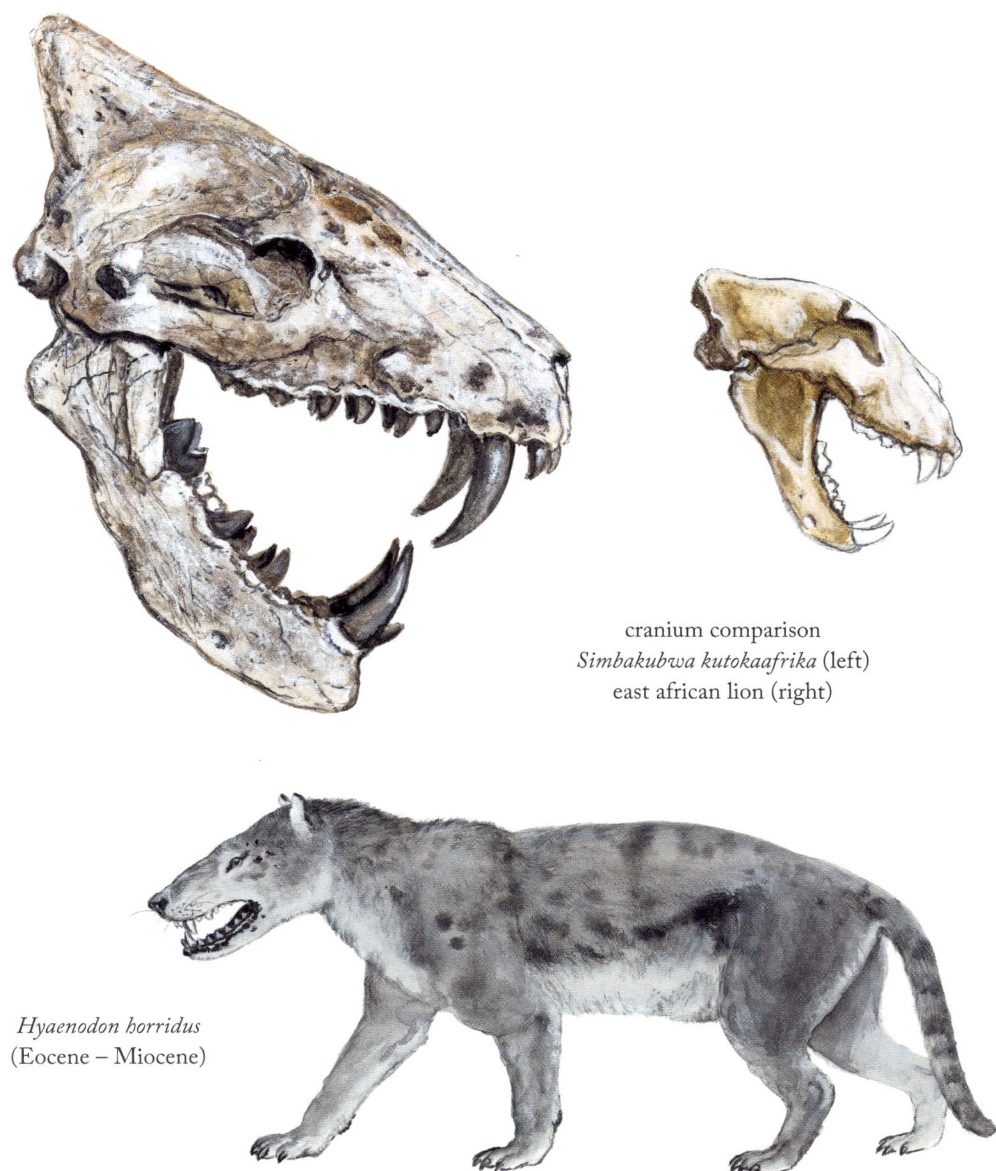

cranium comparison
Simbakubwa kutokaafrika (left)
east african lion (right)

Hyaenodon horridus
(Eocene – Miocene)

HEIGHT: *4 feet*
WEIGHT: *1.5 tons*

Paleontology is incredible because it can make groundbreaking discoveries from fossils long after they were originally found. In 2013, for example, a paleontologist from the University of Ohio named Matthew Borths was researching at the Nairobi National Museum of Kenya. When he asked to inspect the contents of a "hyenas" collection, he was shocked to find jaws, teeth, and skull pieces of an unknown predator that could have been bigger than a polar bear! By the time these remains were discovered and identified, they had been sitting in the museum since the 1970s!

Borths teamed up with his colleague, Nancy Stevens, and they set about analyzing the unusual fossils – which turned out to be 22 million years old! The research results, published in 2019, revealed that a new species of mammal had been discovered in eastern Africa. This species was given the Swahili name *Simbakubwa kutokaafrika*, which means "Great lion of Africa." It lived there about 20 million years ago and was much bigger than today's lions, with a skull comparable in size to that of a rhinoceros. Its strong teeth showed that it was a carnivore. It was also confirmed that it is the largest representative of *Hyaenodonta* (Greek for "hyena teeth"), an extinct genus of predatory mammals. *Hyaenodonts* were dominant predators until they became extinct about 18 million years ago, though the exact cause of their extinction is unknown.

Who would have guessed that such great discoveries could be made in museums? And who can guess what prehistoric surprises still await in the hidden drawers of other museums?

ARGENTAVIS MAGNIFICENS

Cenozoic Era · Miocene

Pelagornis chilensis
(Oligocene – Pleistocene)

Teratornis merriami
(Pleistocene)

Pelagornis chilensis
(Oligocene – Pleistocene)

WINGSPAN: *16–20 feet*
WEIGHT: *Over 155 pounds*

Argentina in South America is an amazing place for paleontologists. It was home to the largest land dinosaurs and the largest known bird in history flew above its plains and mountains. Using the modern scientific view that birds are essentially dinosaurs, due to their having descended from them, Argentina can lay claim to the biggest flying dinosaur: *Argentavis*.

The "magnificent Argentinian bird" (*Argentavis magnificiens*) was scientifically described in 1980, following discoveries made in central and northwest Argentina. Although it was not the largest bird by wingspan, it was certainly the heaviest and most powerful bird capable of powered flight. It could weigh over 155 pounds, and its wingspan was estimated to be between 16 and 19 feet. It was so tall that when standing on the ground, it would have been at eye level with an adult human. We know of a larger wingspan (up to 24 feet) in certain marine birds of the genus *Pelargonis* from the Early Tertiary Period, but these giant birds weighed about 85 pounds – about half as much as *Argentavis*.

Argentavis belonged to the Teratornithidae family of large birds that inhabited the Americas 10,000 years ago. We believe that its legs were strong enough to allow movement on land, giving it a similar appearance and way of life to the condor we know today. However, *Argentavis* had a hooked beak tip, which begs the question of whether it was an active hunter or just a scavenger.

Scientists believe that the *Argentavis* laid a maximum of two eggs every two years. Each egg weighed around two pounds. Remarkably, it took a long time for the *Argentavis* to grow up, not reaching full maturity until it was 12 years old.

It's no easy feat for a big, heavy animal to take off and fly. North American scientists used computer simulations that were originally designed for helicopters to figure out how *Argentavis* could stay in the air with the power of its chest muscles alone. Like modern-day condors, it likely rode on warm air currents. It took off by going downhill into a headwind, the same way people do today on hang-gliders.

When sailing through the sky, it could soar up to 37 miles per hour, gliding through the air for dozens of miles. Some researchers believe that the air was thicker in the past, which could explain why birds of flight were so much larger back then. There are still many mysteries about this creature – and many other ancient birds – that have yet to be solved.

OTODUS MEGALODON

Cenozoic Era · Miocene – Pliocene

size comparison *Otodus megalodon* (top) and white shark

Otodus megalodon jaw

tooth size comparison *Otodus megalodon* (left) and white shark (right)

LENGTH: *53 feet*
WEIGHT: *50 tons*

There are creatures in today's oceans whose sheer size can take our breath away. As far as we know, the largest animal ever to have lived is the modern blue whale. The megalodon, a giant shark whose name means "big tooth," was believed to be almost as large. It fed on large cetaceans. Unfortunately, determining its size is difficult since the megalodon's skeleton was made of cartilage and only its teeth and vertebrae have survived as fossils.

According to the latest mathematical models, an adult megalodon grew to be over 52 feet long and to weigh almost 110,000 pounds. Its dorsal fin was as tall as a human, and its jaws could exert far greater pressure than those of any other animal – with a bite five times stronger than that of a *T. rex*, for example. Filled with saw-like teeth that were five inches long, these deadly jaws spanned over six feet. The megalodon occurred in warmer ocean waters all over the world, as fossil finds testify. It came upon its prey – most notably cetaceans and giant turtles – from below, at tremendous speed. It would stun the prey before stripping it of its fins to prevent its escape.

The megalodon has been known to us for a long time, but scientists still don't know which branch of evolution it belongs to. People used to think its teeth were dragon tongues. In 1843, a Swiss paleontologist named Louis Agassiz gave it a scientific description. It lived in the ocean 23 million years ago in the later Tertiary Period. People used to think it died out 2.6 million years ago due to an ancient ice age, but the most recent research shows it went extinct at least 1 million years earlier. The reason it died out was probably because it couldn't compete with the great white shark for living space. The great white shark is only one-third the size, but it can survive in cold water – and it still exists today.

While scientists know that the megalodon went extinct 3.5 million years ago, and there is no evidence that it is still alive, some people believe otherwise. For example, not long ago, indigenous people from the Hawaiian Islands would perform a ritual with coconut shells to summon the massive "Shark King" that they sometimes encountered. While some people think they saw a megalodon, the simpler – and therefore likelier – explanation is simply that they saw a big modern-day shark.

We still have much to learn about modern-day monsters of the ocean deep. For instance, the 16-foot-long megamouth shark – a deepwater shark rarely seen by people – was not discovered until 1976. Since then, fewer than 100 specimens have been seen or caught.

JOSEPHOARTIGASIA MONESI

Cenozoic Era · Pliocene

pacarana
(*Dinomys branickii*)
(present)

capybara
(*Hydrochoerus hydrochaeris*)
(present)

size comparison
with contemporary
pacaranidae

Josephoartigasia monesi

capybara

pacarana

LENGTH: *10 feet*
WEIGHT: *1 ton*

Today's rodents are mostly small mammals, which is why they make such great pets. But millions of years ago, in South America, there were guinea pigs that were so big they wouldn't have fit in your bedroom!

They weren't exactly guinea pigs, though. They were a relative of the guinea pig called *Josephoartigasia*. The remains of this creature's skull, measuring 20 inches, were found in the 1980s near Montevideo, the capital of Uruguay. It was stored for many years in Uruguay's Natural History Museum, but no one paid it much attention. Not until 2008 was the skull thoroughly investigated – and the results were astonishing. The skull turned out to belong to a rodent as big as a buffalo, weighing around a ton. It was named after José Gervasio Artigas, the father of Uruguayan nationhood.

The genus *Josephoartigasia* is known for two species of similar size, one of which – the pacarana – survives to this day. The pacarana weighs upwards of 30 pounds. The other species, which is extinct, was nine feet long and 4.5 feet tall, with a short tail and two incisors measuring 10 inches long. Scientists believe these teeth were used for digging up roots and plants from swamps, rather than for hunting, and they may have served as a defense against predators. At the time that it was alive, South America was full of predators, such as saber-toothed beasts and giant birds. *Josephoartigasia monesi* likely went extinct after the Great American Interchange, when it couldn't compete with the mammals that had come to South America from the north. The largest rodent today is the capybara, a semiaquatic creature that can weigh up to 175 pounds. Although much smaller than *Josephoartigasia*, its way of life can tell us a lot about the prehistoric creature.

TITANIS WALLERI

Cenozoic Era · Pliocene – Pleistocene

Andalgalornis steulleti (Miocene)

Kelenken guillermoi (Miocene)

Phorusrhacos longissimus (Miocene) cranium

HEIGHT: *Over 8 feet*
WEIGHT: *440 pounds*

South America remained isolated for a long time, which led to the evolution of many unique plants and animals. Without large mammals hunting them, birds filled the role of predators – but not just any birds. These were giant "terror birds."

All "terror birds" belonged to the Phorusrhacidae family, and thus are also called phorusrhacids. Flightless and with stunted wings, they preyed on other vertebrates, which they killed with their huge, axe-like beaks and mighty claws. We believe that they were excellent runners, traveling at higher speeds than the present-day ostrich, making them faster than an Olympic sprinter.

They first appeared in South America shortly after the dinosaurs went extinct, around 62 million years ago. They likely reached their peak development during the Miocene Epoch, between five million and 23 million years ago. Their closest living relative is the much smaller red-legged seriema, which can be found on the grasslands of South America. People even use the seriema as an alternative to a guard dog.

Today we know of about 15 types of phorusrhacids, and there might be more out there waiting to be found. For example, *Kelenken guillermoi* was discovered in Patagonia in 1999. It had the biggest bird skull ever, measuring about 27 inches long, with almost 20 inches of that being its huge beak. Scientists studied the type of phorusrhacid called *Andalgalornis* and discovered in 2010 that they hunted like modern-day boxers, jabbing their prey with their beaks over and over again.

No one has been able to explain why the "terror birds" had hook-like spurs on their legs. Were they used for fighting? Or for mating? We also don't know why these creatures went extinct, but one reason could be the formation of the Isthmus of Panama (a narrow strip of land that connects North and South America) and the Great American Interchange (a time when animals and plants traveled between North and South America, mixing together) about three million years ago. This allowed North American animals to move into South America, replacing the "terror birds." Still, the *Titanis* genus, named after the Titan gods of Ancient Greek mythology, made it through the Isthmus of Panama to the north, where they kept evolving.

Fossils of the species *Titanis walleri*, named after their discoverer Benjamin Waller, were discovered in Florida and Texas in the southern United States. *Titanis* was over eight feet tall and weighed about 440 pounds. The skull of the species has yet to be discovered, but it is presumed to end in a hooked beak, as is the case with other similar species.

Some speculate that these creatures lived alongside early humans, but this idea lacks scientific support. While the "thunderbirds" and "terror birds" on indigenous American totem poles are culturally and spiritually meaningful, they do not depict *Titanis walleri*, which disappeared around 1.8 million years ago – long before any humans arrived on the scene.

GIGANTOPITHECUS BLACKI

Cenozoic Era · Pliocene – Pleistocene

Gigantopithecus blacki
(Miocene – Pleistocene)

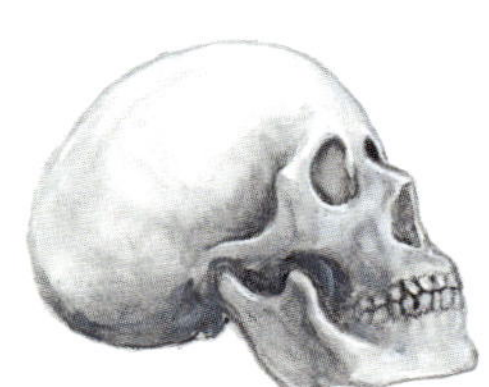

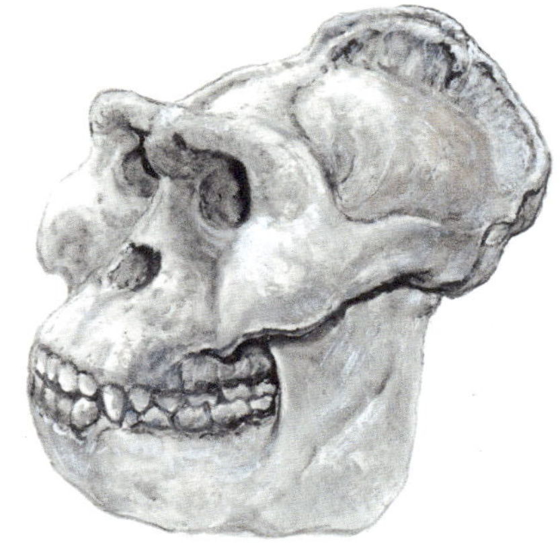

Homo sapiens (left) and
Gigantopithecus blacki (right)
cranium size comparison

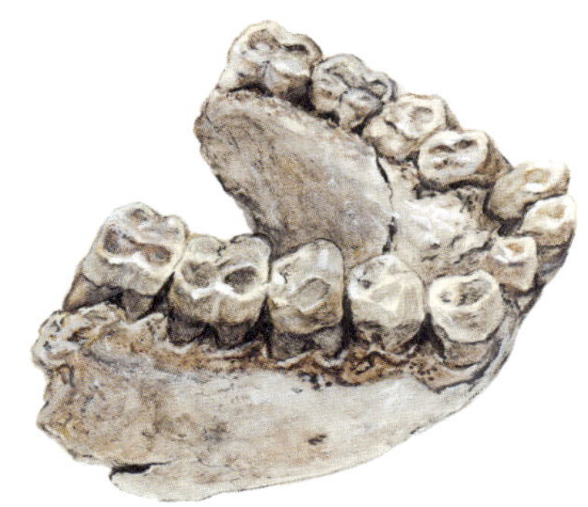

Gigantopithecus blacki
lower jaw

HEIGHT: *10 feet*
WEIGHT: *1,200 pounds*

You have probably heard of the mysterious yeti, also known as the Abominable Snowman. This mythological caveman-like creature is said to be over eight feet tall and is said to live in the Himalayas. Although experts doubt its existence, some believe it could be *Gigantopithecus*, the largest great ape the world has ever seen. The problem with this speculation is that we humans evolved around 150,000 years after *Gigantopithecus* went extinct.

We know very little about the extinct giant primate *Gigantopithecus*. The first description of this species came in 1935, when German-Dutch paleontologist Ralph von Koenigswald found an unusually large molar in a Chinese pharmacy in Hong Kong. It was being sold as a dragon's tooth, a traditional Chinese medicine. Von Koenigswald named the species *Gigantopithecus blacki*, in honor of Canadian paleontologist Davidson Black. Later, smaller and older specimens were found in other Asian locations and were named *Gigantopithecus giganthea*.

The size of the tooth suggests that *Gigantopithecus* was almost 10 feet tall and weighed around 1,200 pounds, making it a whopping *three times* bigger than today's gorillas. Because of its size, it probably lived and moved around on the ground on all fours, instead of swinging from tree to tree. In 2019, an analysis of protein taken from its tooth enamel showed its closest living relative to be the orangutan, leading us to believe it may have had a reddish-brown coat. This protein was studied using proteomics, a method that is likely to make more such amazing discoveries in the field of paleontology in the near future.

The thickness of the tooth enamel shows that this creature was an herbivore (plant-eater) who liked crunchy foods like bamboo and tree branches. It's possible that it didn't evolve with the changing climate fast enough and died out. Another idea is that competition from the giant panda edged it out of existence. Ancestors of modern-day humans were competitors of *Gigantopithecus* too; they shared a living space with it for a million years. While it is unlikely that these proto-humans hunted *Gigantopithecus*, they occupied its territory and used its bamboo.

DIPROTODON OPTATUM

Cenozoic Era · Pleistocene

HEIGHT: *6.5 feet*
WEIGHT: *3 tons*

Australia, the world's smallest continent, is home to many unique animal and plant species due to its isolation. Its prehistory has revealed fossils of creatures not found anywhere else. The Pleistocene megafauna, of which *Diprotodon* was the largest marsupial ever, flourished here. Other remarkable creatures roamed the Australian mainland before *Diprotodon*. The kangaroo has undergone a weird and wonderful evolution: there once existed carnivorous species as well as a short-nosed one that specialized in eating less digestible parts of plants. Its skull is similar to that of the modern panda, indicating a similar lifestyle. The largest kangaroo, *Procoptodon*, was up to 9 feet in length and 530 pounds in weight. Early marsupials included predators, such as the Tasmanian wolf, which died out in the 20th century. *Thylacoleo carnifex*, an enormous marsupial carnivore, attacked from the trees and had cat-like retractable claws, which marsupials otherwise don't have.

The cuddly koala has an enormous relative – a prehistoric marsupial called *Nimbadon*. It lived in a similar way to the koala, but it could weigh up to 175 pounds! Discovered in 2012, *Nimbadon* lived in the ancient forests of Australia 15 million years ago. As well as giant marsupials, prehistoric Australia was home to *Dromornis*, a flightless bird related to geese that was up to nine feet tall and weighed over 1,000 pounds. There was also *Megalania* (*Varanus priscus*), the largest lizard ever, related to the Komodo dragon, which was up to 23 feet long. *Megalania* may have even hunted *Diprotodon*.

Diprotodon was related to the wombat, but it looked more like a rhinoceros without a horn. At 6.5 feet tall and 10 feet long, it weighed 6,500 pounds and lived in Australia 1.8 million years ago. Its name comes from Ancient Greek and means "two protruding front teeth" because of its large, ever-growing incisors. It used these to nibble on plants like a rabbit, and its mighty claws were used to get to the roots. Like elephants, it traveled in herds over long distances in search of food.

The Aboriginal Australian legend of the bunyip may have been inspired by the bones of *Diprotodon*. Unlike the bunyip, *Diprotodon* wasn't dangerous to humans – in fact, humans were dangerous to *Diprotodon*. About 50,000 years ago, when humans first arrived in Australia, this animal and others in this chapter quickly disappeared. Primitive weapons, the use of fire, and the clearing of rainforests for fields were human achievements that these unique animals couldn't survive. There is also a theory that their extinction was due to climate change.

HOMO FLORESIENSIS

Cenozoic Era · Pleistocene

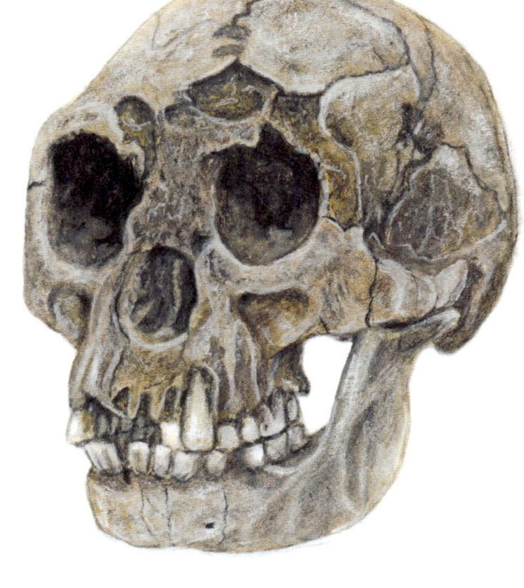

head and cranium

HEIGHT: *3.5 feet*
WEIGHT: *66 pounds*

Believe it or not, modern humans like you and me aren't the only species of humans to have existed. Neanderthals, a well-known ancient human group that was shorter but larger than us, not only coexisted with our ancestors but also interbred with them. Additionally, there is another intriguing species, *Homo floresiensis*, commonly known as "Hobbits." Discovered on the Indonesian island of Flores, these small-statured humans have sparked ongoing debates among scientists. The genetic legacy of Neanderthals is particularly evident in present-day Europeans, who carry a small percentage of Neanderthal DNA, underscoring the intricate relationships between different human species throughout our evolutionary past.

The island of Flores is located off the coast of Indonesia's Lesser Sunda Islands, and due to a deep trench, it was not affected much by the Ice Age. This made it possible for settlers to reach the island by water. Archeologist Michael Morwood was curious to find out who the first settlers were, so he conducted his research in a rock overhang called Liang Bua ("cold cave"). Morwood's exploration went deeper than his predecessors, and on September 2, 2003, he discovered a skull and skeletal parts that were about three feet tall. This discovery astonished the scientific world, and Australian expert Peter Brown created a scientific description of the species. The most striking thing about it was the small size of the skull.

Homo floresiensis is an example of an evolutionary phenomenon called insular dwarfism, in which creatures – even human ones – get smaller due to limited food sources. Scientists have nicknamed these small humans "hobbits" and believe they lived on the island as recently as 11,800 years ago – around the time modern humans invented agriculture. Some scientists are skeptical about this, as Indonesian paleontologist Teuku Jacob damaged the bones while investigating. He thought it was not a new species but an individual with a medical condition called microcephaly, in which the brain is abnormally small.

Many questions remain about the development of *Homo floresiensis*. To date, only about ten other skeletal remains of "Flores Man" have been found on the island, none as complete as the first. Despite this, some of the features of *Homo floresiensis* (like the small head) are similar to those of our ancient ancestors, while the jaw is very up-to-date in terms of evolution. It's thought that the first members of the species may have left the mainland on rafts after a volcanic eruption (the area is known for its seismic activity), so that they could survive.

Its size may have been reduced in the same way as that of *Stegodon*, a dwarfish elephant that was also endemic to Flores, and thus was the prey of *Homo floresiensis*. As was the case with the giant turtle, such hunting probably brought about *Stegodon*'s extinction.

Having colonized the island 700,000 years ago (according to the latest research), *Homo floresiensis* could itself have become the prey of another animal.

For thousands of years, people believed that modern humans caused the extinction of Flores Man. However, recent evidence suggests that a volcanic eruption about 12,000 years ago was the real culprit. The "hobbit" is still remembered in the stories of local people as a hairy little creature called Ebu Gogo. Some ethnologists even think that tales about Ebu Gogo might date back to memories of actual encounters between modern humans and *Homo floresiensis.*

SMILODON POPULATOR

Cenozoic Era · Pleistocene – Holocene

Thylacosmilus atrox
(Pliocene)

Smilodon populator
(Pleistocene)
cranium

Barbourofelis fricki
(Miocene – Pliocene)

HEIGHT: *3.3 feet*
WEIGHT: *350–660 pounds*

Smilodon is the scientific name for the saber-toothed tiger, one of the most famous prehistoric predators. While we can't be 100 percent sure what its giant fangs were used for – certainly not for chewing – one plausible theory is that they were used to deliver a fatal ripping wound to its prey.

According to current classifications, the genus *Smilodon* has three species. *Smilodon* first appeared about 2.5 million years ago and is unrelated to modern tigers. The eastern part of South America was home to *Smilodon populator*, one of the largest cats ever known. Its heaviest members weighed 880 pounds and its upper canines were nearly 12 inches long. In 1834, Danish naturalist Peter Wilhelm Lund discovered these canines in caves in Brazil and gave them a scientific description. He also gave the creature its Latin name, which means "double-edged tooth" – an apt name for the animal, which was smaller than a tiger but just as strong and powerful, with a build more like a bear.

Smilodon had a much weaker bite force than today's big cats, and this is linked to their different hunting strategies. Instead of strangling its prey, *Smilodon* would first press it to the ground with its huge front paws and then stab it with its huge but relatively fragile canine teeth. It's thought that it killed quickly, by slicing its prey's carotid artery.

It is also thought that *Smilodon* hunted in packs, though there is no definite proof. Its prey likely included bison, elk, tapirs, mastodons, and giant ground sloths. The most famous *Smilodon* discovery site is the La Brea Tar Pits in Los Angeles, where remains of up to 3,000 saber-toothed tigers, as well as other old animals, have been found. This area contains several natural asphalt lakes, and the asphalt rises to the surface. An oily, sticky black substance that's hard to break free of, asphalt killed many mammoths that wandered into it in search of food. Over the course of thousands of years, herbivores and their predators were also drawn into the pits. Asphalt is an excellent preserver, though, so the finds from these pits (many of which are on display) give us a good snapshot of how North America's ecosystem looked in the distant past.

We still don't know for sure why *Smilodon* went extinct, but it likely had to do with its hunting style and its favorite prey of large plant-eaters. When the climate changed at the end of the last Ice Age and those plant-eaters died out, *Smilodon* had no food. People may have also had a hand in *Smilodon*'s disappearance, likely by killing them and/or spreading sickness.

MEGATHERIUM AMERICANUM

Cenozoic Era · Pliocene – Holocene

Macrauchenia patagonica
(Paleocene – Pleistocene)

Glyptodon reticulatus
(Pleistocene)

Scelidotherium leptocephalum
(Pleistocene)

HEIGHT: *20 feet*
WEIGHT: *6 tons*

You might be surprised to learn that even though modern-day sloths and armadillos are fairly small animals, their prehistoric ancestors were much bigger than today's elephants! And the biggest of these ancient animals was the *Megatherium Americanum*. At 20 feet long and weighing up to 12,000 pounds, it used its long claws and tail to stand up and grab branches to eat leaves. It was so big that it was actually taller than the very trees it ate from. Studies of *Megatherium* tracks discovered at the now famous site of Pehuen Có on the Atlantic coast in Argentina have led some scientists to conclude that it walked on its hind limbs only.

In 1986, tracks of large mammals, including the three-foot-long *Glyptodon* (an armadillo relative), a huge bird related to the rhea, and the Macrauchenia (a large hoofed herbivore) were found at Pehuen Có. While Charles Darwin had discovered *Macrauchenia* remains in Patagonia in the 19th century, these new tracks offered new insights. All of the tracks were estimated to be around 12,000 years old, and all the above-mentioned species had one thing in common: they became extinct around 10,000 BCE, as a result of climate change. *Megatherium* was unable to survive the disappearance of wide-open steppes and their replacement by dense forests. This change also coincided with the arrival of human settlers from the north. Humans are most likely responsible for the extinction of certain large native species here – and unfortunately, elsewhere around the world.

The influence of human intervention on *Megatherium* has yet to be fully established, although we know for sure that it was hunted by humans. Early American Indians were pretty good at figuring out what bones belonged to extinct animals, and they called *Megatherium* "thunder horses." They also named another incredible animal from long ago, *Megacerops*, which was like a rhinoceros and died out 30,000 years ago. They called it "large horn face."

COELODONTA ANTIQUITATIS

Cenozoic Era · Pleistocene – Holocene

Elasmotherium sibiricum
(Pleistocene)

cave painting of a woolly rhinoceros,
Rouffignac cave, Dordogne, France

Stephanorhinus (dicerorhinus) etruscus
(Pleistocene)

LENGTH: *13 feet*
WEIGHT: *5 tons*

You wouldn't want to stumble across a rhinoceros in the wild – although considering that humans have tragically brought the present-day rhino to the brink of extinction, the chance of that happening is low. However, an encounter between a human and a rhino – a woolly rhino, that is – would have been fairly common 10,000 years ago. And because that was during the Ice Age, it makes sense that the woolly rhino had a thick fur coat.

The woolly rhinoceros was one of the most recognizable animals of the Pleistocene Epoch. It was known to early humans, as evidenced by cave paintings. In fact, these paintings show a fairly accurate depiction of the rhino, which had a large, four-foot-long body, short stubby legs, external ears, and two horns, with the front horn growing up to a foot in length. It is believed that the largest woolly rhinos weighed around five tons. They ate plants they dug from the snow-covered steppe with their horns and were well-protected from the harsh weather of their habitat by their thick, waterproof fur.

For a long time, scientists thought the woolly rhino evolved during the last Ice Age, which is when most of our fossils of it are from. But recent research has found that the woolly rhino lived three million years ago on the Tibetan Plateau, where it had the opportunity to get used to the cold. It then spread out to other areas when much of central Europe was covered in snow and ice.

During the Middle Ages – way back in 1335, to be precise – a piece of a woolly rhinoceros skull was discovered in Central Europe. And it has been kept in the Austrian city of Klagenfurt ever since. Originally thought to be part of a "dragon's head," this fossil is the oldest known paleontological find. Humans may have played a part in the extinction of the woolly rhinoceros, as well as the woolly mammoth, but recent studies suggest that climate change and the melting of ice dealt this species a far heavier blow.

Although the woolly rhinoceros was quite big, it was nowhere near as big as some of its relatives. For example, Elasmotherium, which lived in the same area and time, had a seven-foot-long horn on its head and weighed up to seven tons. And that's nothing compared to the hornless rhino Paraceratherium, which you can learn more about in this book.

MEGALOCEROS GIGANTEUS

Cenozoic Era · Pliocene – Pleistocene

Cervalces scotti
(Pleistocene – Holocene)

Megaloceros
hunting game of prehistoric people

HEIGHT: *6.6 feet*
WEIGHT: *1,500 pounds*

The most impressive antlers ever seen on Earth surely belonged to the Irish elk, the largest deer-like ungulate that has ever lived. Fossil remains have been found all over Eurasia, allowing scientists to accurately recreate it. It stood about seven feet tall, was 10 feet long, and its antlers spanned 12 feet. Combined, the two antlers weighed 90 pounds. We may never know why the Irish elk had such huge antlers, but they might have been used to attract a mate, like today's stags. This would make sense, as the antlers would have made it difficult to move around in the forest, suggesting it lived a solitary life in open plains, steppes, and tundra.

The Irish elk, also called the Irish deer or giant deer, is thus named because the best-preserved fossils of this creature, and the earliest descriptions of it, come from Ireland in the late 17th century. It was most commonly found in Siberia, though, and evidence suggests it still lived there as recently as 4,500 years ago, meaning it would have interacted with prehistoric humans.

In fact, prehistoric hunters may well have been partly responsible for the extinction of the Irish elk. It disappeared quickly at the end of the last Ice Age. One possible reason was its huge antlers – climate change caused the area to become forested and the ground to become softer, making it easier for hunters to spot and catch the elk.

In 2009, though, American scientists proposed a new theory for why the Irish elk went extinct. They argued that the male's huge antlers weren't a factor, as they had time to evolve to be smaller in order for the Irish elk to survive. Instead, these scientists looked at the female and the reproduction of the species, and concluded that climate change had caused food shortages, leading to their extinction.

Scan the QR code for
more information and sources.

5. května 1746/22, Prague 4, Czech Republic
Author: Radek Malý
Illustrator: Petr Modlitba
Translator: Andrew Oakland
Editor: Scott Alexander Jones

www.albatrosbooks.com

Printed in China by Leo Paper Group.

albatros_books_

Albatros Books

Albatros Books US